Russia
Women Tha...

Oksana Boichenko

and

Maria Derevyanko

FREE OFFERS FROM OKSANA BOICHENKO

TO HELP YOU MEET QUALITY WOMEN TODAY

<u>Special Free Gift # 1 from the Author:</u>

FREE WALL CALENDAR WITH THE MOST BEAUTIFUL WOMEN MEN LIVE FOR WHOM YOU ARE ENTITLED TO MEET

In the Calendar you will see real most Alluring women you can ask out on a DATE TODAY.

Visit www.OksanaLove.com/GIFT to register your free profile and enter promo code **FREE416** in the "Promo Code" field to get:

1. Your free wall calendar with 12 beautiful Russian women of my agency (shipped to your door).

2. The ULTIMATE Insider Secrets booklet containing in depth background information about all 12 women (shipped with the calendar).

Special Free Gift # 2 from the Author:

FREE FIRST CHAPTER OF THE BOOK

Russian Allure: "SCAM ME NOT"

Revealed in the book:

- 3 most popular sites where you will run into scammers.
- 2 most frequently used scam schemes
- Training boot camp that creates professional scammers
- Scammer profiles
- Inside operations of scam agencies
- Letter templates con artists use to get your money
- "Wages" of scammers
- 7 simple steps to check if your Russian woman is real
- How to determine the difference between a real Russian Allure and a fake

And much more.

Meet my guest # 1 **Interview in the book**– a scam agency manager Kate. She has been scamming men just like you for many years, and today she will reveal the naked truth of what's happening inside this "business" and how scammers operate to squeeze funds out of men just like you.

The information included in the book is a MUST HAVE resource for every man who is considering finding a beautiful Russian wife.
Go to www.OksanaLove.com/rbscam and enter your email to claim your free gift - first chapter of the book "Scam me NOT". You will also be automatically enrolled to win a free copy of my book.

"There's nothing better- looking than a good-looking Russian woman. "

Diana Vreeland

Style editor and Harper's Bazaar 1936-1962
and editor in chief of Vogue 1963-1971

Ms. Vreeland's love of anything beautiful and distaste for the pedestrian.

There's only one very good life and that's the life you know you want and you make it yourself. Within every girl in Russia is the possibility of arousing emotion. Without emotion there is no beauty. You know the greatest thing is passion, without it what have you got? I mean if you love someone you can love them as much as you can love them but if it isn't a passion, it isn't burning, and it isn't on fire: you haven't lived.

And you haven't lived if you are not married to a Russian woman who is not passionate about you. Which is what I can do for you better than anyone else in the world…to help you find that one beautiful Russian woman you were born to love and be with. Yours dream of having loving and passionate relationship doesn't have to be just a dream. You are entitled to have it your reality.

Manolo Blahnik once stated "You put high heels on, you change". In Russia every women wears high heels everyday of her life for everything she does…which is perhaps what makes her so emotionally passionate to be with….

INTRODUCTION

This book could have been called "**90 days to a happy marriage**" - the less poetic name because, according to the US government requirements, that's all you have to marry your true love. Yes, you read it right – when you bring someone from abroad to your country, you only have 90 days to become closely acquainted, get engaged, plan your wedding, and get married. Not very romantic, but that's what you got. Not a day more, not a minute more, not a second more – you have 90 days to establish your relationship and create a happy marriage.

While you will say goodbye to romantic encounters, your life will become more exciting through many other experiences, you will look at things you've taken for granted in a new way. I remember my first week in the USA. I remember my first visit to McDonald's. You see, in my country, Kazakhstan, we didn't have McDonalds (and still don't), so for me the drive-through experience at McDonald's was equal to a restaurant visit. I was happy like a child while sitting in the passenger seat, looking at the menu pictures, pulling up to the window, and getting a friendly greeting from the cashier. Why? Because being served with a smile was not something I could expect in my country. I went through McDonald's drive-through every chance I had (oh, the excitement of beautiful menus, cute condiments, and delicious cheeseburgers I never knew existed!); that was an experience I would never forget. I've lived in America for 15 years and eventually, just like you, I found little excitement in going through the drive-through at McDonald's until I had a visit from my Kazakhstan friends who reminded me how exciting such experience can be to someone who's never had it before. Little things like this change the way we see our life, it becomes interesting and exciting when you see it through someone else's eyes.

How do I know that creating a happy family in 90 days is possible? I know this because it happened to me. I came to this country with a dream to create a family; I was willing to give up romance, a beautiful wedding, having my parents by my side during the ceremony for the sake of creating a happy future with the man I loved. And I am not an exception – there are hundreds of women who followed their dream to come to America and were married before their 90 days were up.

In fact, during my 17 years of working as a personal matchmaker, I've seen people making it happen in much less time. I've tested the possibility of finding a perfect woman for my clients and have the two get married in 90 days more than once and included all my findings in the matchmaking program "90 days: life transformation system."

As you see, the strategy I offer you in this book is based on many years of experience. I do more than offer dating advice – I give you marriage oriented advice to help you build a happy family and make your union with the woman of your dreams successful. The reason most of my clients come to me is to meet a sincere, authentic, drama-free, considerate, beautiful, educated, feminine, passionate, driven, unique woman with whom they can create a solid relationship based on traditional family values – and they do. They get tangible, quality results through meeting and finding the right woman and building a serious relationship without wasting their time and efforts in empty pursuits. Now I offer the same package to you: I will help you find and meet a real woman who will fulfill your dreams and become a part of your life through marriage (I can already imagine how jealous all your friends will be!).

There is a catch though. When looking for that perfect Russian woman, you have to be able to make quick decisions because it is too easy to miss perfect opportunities. I've seen it happen many times: while a man takes his time making a decision about his future pursuits, the woman he likes meets someone else who sees her for the treasure she is, and becomes involved in a serious relationship. In fact, the same goes for Russian and Eastern European women who currently live in the United States. Basically, if you snooze, you lose. However, since you are reading this book, I know you will avoid this pitfall.

So, we are going to focus on 90 days. I will give you exact steps to follow so that you can meet your true love, the woman of your dreams with whom you might want to share your life. I offer you a balanced system; if you follow its core concepts, I guarantee results. All these principles and concepts are easy to apply:

1) Know what type of a woman you want in your life (yes, it's quite all right to want to find a beautiful, smart woman!);
2) Know where you can find her;
3) Make the right moves to make her fall in love with you and make her want to spend the rest of her life with you.

This book will give you answers to all these questions. And, if you begin following my advice now instead of waiting for better times, 90 days from now you will tell me that you have someone special in your life. In fact, if you use just a quarter of the information from this book, it will improve your communication and relationship building skills with any woman. I will make an even bigger claim: some of this information may save you thousands of dollars and many hours of using the wrong dating services, writing to the wrong women, and visiting the wrong places.

Last word of caution: dating a Russian woman is not for anyone – you will have to go above and beyond your usual dating efforts; you might have to change some of the core ideas you have about women, dating, and building a relationship; you will definitely have to adjust and keep an open mind. If you are prepared for this and think you have what it takes to find your perfect "Russian woman", this book is definitely for you. All right! Ready, set, go!

CHAPTER 1: BEFORE IT ALL BEGINS

Starting your search for a Russian bride, or "would you like fries with that?"

Before you begin your search for a Russian bride, you need to be aware of a very important thing that can make or break any attempt to meet a decent woman from abroad. You may have heard and even used the term "mail order bride", but if you are serious about finding a wife overseas, you need to forget it once and for all. You are not browsing through a catalog to have an item shipped to you, you are not shopping for an accessory, and you simply cannot order a person!

Political correctness aside, if you use this term while communicating with Russian women, most of them will refuse to talk to you as to them this term is insulting. Women I can introduce you to are respectful and well established; they have pride and know their worth. To call them a "mail order bride" is to show them disrespect and flaunt your ignorance. They might forgive you, but they will never consider you a potential partner.

Some men are arrogant and uneducated enough to think that any Russian woman would want to be with them simply because they carry an American or a European passport – they are hugely mistaken. If you are one of them, put this book aside now because in order to win a Russian woman's heart you must be respectful of other cultures. Please, keep in mind – you have to EARN your woman, and in the following chapters of this book I will tell you HOW to do it.

Are you man enough?

Being with a Russian woman is not for everyone. Neither is international dating. It doesn't matter why you are interested in Russian women – dating someone who lives halfway across the world will test your patience and dedication more than once. Long distance relationships might be great in many ways, but they are harder to manage than a traditional relationship. Still, international relationships are a lot of fun, and when your woman will finally arrive to your country, both of you will say that being together was definitely worth the wait.

Often men choose international dating because it is a "convenient" option, half the time they don't have any intention of turning their communication into "the real thing". If both partners have this attitude, you can do as you please, but if you are the only one to see it that way, you would be giving false hopes to the person on the receiving end. In other words, if you are only interested in a pen pal instead a wife and a lifetime partner, look elsewhere.

Before you start dating a Russian woman, settle any unfinished issues with other women in your life. It is not uncommon for men to join Russian dating websites and even visit Russian women while they are in fact simply separated from their wives or are on a break from an ongoing relationship. Dating someone from abroad might seem like a safe option at such times, but you will only complicate your own life and, quite possibly, seriously hurt someone's feelings.

International dating is an option only for secure people. If you are the jealous type, it will never work for you because you will be constantly questioning your partner and wondering what your Russian lady is up to now. I've been a witness to many instances of serious interrogations by men when their women would not be available for a spontaneous phone call, for example. Despite perfectly legitimate reasons, women would end up being questioned up one side and down the other, while a distraught guy would be pulling his hair out with frustration from all suspicions circling in his head.

You also must consider the issue of travel if you decide to date a Russian woman. Men often want to bring a woman to their country for the first meeting. While this is an option, it is not always easy to accomplish this for a number of reasons: your woman might have difficulty getting a visa for her trip, she might feel unsafe coming to stay with someone she's never met, and you will not have an opportunity to get to know her in her own surrounding. If you are not capable of visiting your potential bride in her country, you might consider planning a meeting on a neutral territory. Whatever the case, you must be prepared to sponsor your lady as she might not be able to afford the trip. Naturally, make sure you have a valid passport for when you finally decide to travel.

Dating blind

The beginning of your international dating experience might seem as easy as filling out a profile on an introduction site, but it requires a good deal of preparation – you must have a dating plan before you sit down in front of the computer. In other words, you need to know what you are looking for before diving into hundreds of profiles of gorgeous women. You have to be specific and honest with yourself about your wants, demands, and preferences.

The best way to organize your thoughts is to write down everything you would want in a partner. Be as specific as you can: height, color of hair and eyes, her likes/dislikes, habits, family situation, and anything else you can think of. Don't limit yourself – dare to dream and write down as many things as you like; don't take this lightly – this is done to find out what YOU want and will become the base for the success of your search. Once you have listed all you might want in a partner, prioritize the points you made to make your search fast and easy, but flexible.

You don't have to do this, of course, but if you begin your search without a clear idea of what kind of woman you want to be with, you will end up wasting a lot of time and effort by communicating with dozens attractive women who will not satisfy your needs in a relationship. Trust me, I've seen it happen!

In later chapters I will reveal exactly how you can recognize your ideal woman and how you can stay focused on your goal of meeting her resulting in success of your dating journey. This is why the rest of this book will tell you what you need to do and how to do it the best way possible.

CHAPTER 2: THE MYSTERY OF RUSSIAN WOMEN

America vs. Russia: it's more than politics

Now I am going to make an arrogant claim – if you have ever dated a Russian woman or were married to one, you will NEVER go back to women of your own country. That's a guarantee! While some principles are universal for women all over the world (afternoon tea with girlfriends, shopping, spa visits), cultural and societal influences have created very clear character distinctions between Russian and Western women.

Sex appeal and femininity. If you've ever visited Russia or any other Former Soviet Union country, you have certainly noticed the way women there are dressed and groomed: high heels and mini-skirts are a common sight, and you have to look for women without makeup. A Russian woman will never wear sweatpants when stepping outside the house (in fact, she is not likely to wear them inside the house either).

But the difference between Russian and Western women is more than skin deep. Russian women don't go to all that effort just to see a pretty reflection in the mirror – they like to look sexy for the man they are with. And the sex appeal extends beyond the façade: Russian women know how to keep romance alive and will never punish their man by withholding sex unlike Western women.

Beauty and brains. This combination is more a rule than an exception; most women are in great shape, intelligent, educated, and well-rounded.

Education. Education is taken seriously in Russia. The school system gives children a wider knowledge base than American schools, for example, and there are more people with university degrees than without.

Healthy lifestyle. This comes naturally due to living conditions: women walk a lot because most people don't have cars; they eat home cooked food (and it is good!) since restaurants are considered expensive. As a result, diet and sports are not as popular as they are in the West simply because there is no need for it.

Personality. The main qualities of Russian women are their patience and tolerance. Some things these women can forgive and cope with are more than any Western woman will be ready to bear. Striking a compromise comes naturally, and they generally will do anything it takes to save a relationship. Russian women are generally more considerate and reliable; they look to form a partnership in a relationship, not a competition, as has become common in the West.

Motherhood. Russian women truly are natural-born mothers and keepers of the hearth, full of care and warmth which they are ready to share with their loved ones. In fact, you can expect their affection to extend well past you – they will gladly shower your family with their care as well.

Consideration. It is typical for Russian women to think about others more than about their family and children) for so long that they have it engraved in their minds.

Responsibility. This quality comes naturally – Russian women bear a lot of responsibility on different levels of society and expect little assistance from men. Their sense of responsibility is so great that most Russian women will stay with their husbands even if they would be better off without one (many Russian men drink and mistreat their women). These women can move mountains, but they will never brag about it as many Western women do by claiming their rights and independence.

Action without drama. Russian women will not blow things out of proportion. Life has taught them to cope easily with any situation. These women mature early because they learn responsibility from an early age; they prefer action to drama. When Russian women face challenges, they turn their mind to the task at hand instead of looking for ways to escape the problem; once a Russian woman tackles the issue, she will never brag about what she has accomplished because to her it is the way thing should be.

Being serious and straightforward. You will notice that Russian women stay serious more and smile less than Western women. This happens for two reasons: they generally face difficulties in life from an early age and also don't want to be taken lightly. Their serious manner of communication often leads Western men to believe that women are not interested, but the only way to really know what your Russian woman thinks or feels is to ask her. Russian women can be rather blunt in their statements, and if you present her with a straight-forward question, you will get a straight-forward answer.

Traditional. Russian women are traditional and will expect a man to make the first move. They will not approach you first and, frequently, will not even show their interest. Western men often get confused while trying to figure out whether a particular woman is interested in a relationship. Also, men quickly move on if they don't see obvious signs of a woman's interest (flirting, being forward) instead of discussing the issue directly to find out what she feels.

Faithfulness. Russian women are very forgiving of unfaithfulness from their spouses; they prefer to forgive than to break up. This happens because many women are insecure or because they think they will not find a better man (some women say: "better a cheater, than a beater"). However, it is common for Russian women who have come to live in America to change their views overtime and become less tolerant of unfaithfulness.

For richer or poorer. When a Russian woman marries a man, she really plans to spend her life with him. I recently had a conversation with a friend of mine who is a lawyer – despite the economic crisis, his practice is booming, and most of his money comes from handling divorce. With many families facing financial difficulties in America, many women are leaving their husbands because they are not earning as much money or because they have lost the source of income. This is something that will never happen if you are married to a Russian woman. In fact, your relationship will become stronger, because your Russian woman will stand by your side and work with you to overcome challenges and bring stability to your life.

These claims are not idle praise of Russian women – knowing about these traits and cultural specifics will help you understand their communication style and avoid some common problems in your relationship.

Many faces of Russian women

Foreigners often think that women are the same on the entire territory of the former Soviet Union, but there are many differences between women from different regions – from appearance to mentality and lifestyle. Here is your brief guide to the many faces of Russian women.

Ukraine

Ukrainian women are considered to be the most beautiful women on the territory of the former Soviet Union. Sadly, difficult life

conditions have caused many of them to learn how to use their looks for their own benefit – that is why you hear about so many scammers from Ukraine. However, not all Ukrainian women are scammers, many of them are genuinely interested in finding a husband and creating a family.

------------------------------- Resource! -----------------------------------

To find out how to avoid becoming a scam victim, visit www.OksanaLove.com/rbscam and enter your email to claim your free gift - first chapter of the book "Scam me NOT". Also, you will be automatically enrolled to win a free copy of my book

----

Kazakhstan, Uzbekistan, Kirgizstan

These countries are a part of Central Asia, so Asian culture has had a strong influence on women from these areas; they are very different from women in any other FSU country. Kazakhstani women, for example, combine traditional qualities of Asian women with many modern views of Eastern European women. You will find these women traditional in their views, raised to respect their men and treat them as kings. At the same time, living in a modern country, these women must have an excellent level of education and be able to speak a foreign language to get a good job. Truthfully speaking, I believe that women of Kazakhstan make the best wives (and it isn't just because I am originally from this country).

Russia

Russia is so vast that you will see a big difference even between women from different cities. I give you a brief description of women from three large cities of Russia: Moscow, being the largest, Saint-Petersburg, and Novosibirsk.

Native townswomen of Moscow (as opposed to people who relocated to the city from other areas of the country) are very proud to be called Muscovites. Such women generally consider those who were not born in Moscow foreigners, strangers, and, often, low class representatives. Many such women are lazy when it comes to family life and think they are God's gift to men. It is rather challenging to communicate with such women. With Moscow being the most expensive city in a world (they beat Tokyo a few years ago), you can expect women from this city to expect royal treatment all the time, including extravagantly expensive gifts that can equal your mortgage payment (yes, they do receive such gifts regularly from Russian men!). If you are looking for a woman in Moscow, make sure that she is not a native, but relocated to the city later in life.

Saint-Petersburg women are quite different from Muscovites. The city is considered a cultural capital of Russia due to numerous museums, architectural memorials, libraries, theatres, and other similar establishments. Most women who were born and raised here have one or more university degrees, speak several languages, have excellent manners, and are true ladies who consider themselves nearly royalty. They do not tolerate people without manners and will never give the time of day to a man who doesn't know how to court a woman.

Novosibirsk, the second largest city in Russia, is a well-developed industrial city located in Siberia. Because of living in cold conditions most of the time, women of Novosibirsk have white skin and look 10-20 years younger than their age. However, they are also rather cold when it comes to their character – such women are generally more reserved and cautious in communication, but great people once you get to know them. Generally women from Novosibirsk lead comfortable lives, make decent money, and like to travel to warm places. Since the number of men in the city is a lot less than the number of women, ladies from Novosibirsk get very lonely, but they won't jump into your arms right away – it takes them time to warm up to people. Travelling to Novosibirsk is more challenging than going to Moscow or Saint-Petersburg, however, if you are after blondes with blue eyes, about 70% of women in this city would perfectly match your criteria.

Naturally, I can't tell you about every city and village in that corner of the world, but at least you know that women from different areas can vary in character and mentality quite a bit. Now that you know about these differences, you can make your communication with Russian women more effective – you know not to stereotype them and can adjust your communication accordingly.

What your Russian bride can do for you

As I have already said, the search for your Russian bride is really just the beginning. Her arrival to your country is when you finally get to the good stuff – sharing many wonderful experiences, discovering new angles of your relationship, and getting to know each other even better. It will also be the time of change for both of you – for her more so than you. Being exposed to a different culture will certainly transform her views and preferences, but, in my experience, these changes are usually for the best.

Your Russian wife will most likely direct her sense of great responsibility and ability to work hard towards her home, family, and/or career. Intelligence and persistence allow most Russian women to learn the language quickly, to find and succeed in a job, as well as to maintain an immaculate home with ease and smile. Most women married to foreigners see living abroad as a way to be free: financially, emotionally, and spiritually. Many Russian women say that moving abroad has given them the chance to do the things they had always dreamt about doing (travelling, helping family, pursuing personal interests), but they are also ready to work for it.

If your woman has the mind of an entrepreneur, especially if she had a business at home, she will generally follow the same path in the new country and can often achieve even greater results due to having more opportunities. When such women marry somebody without much money, they readily invest in their partner's life and strive to improve it and make more satisfying. Russian women are very generous and are generally ready to share if they believe that a man's intentions are sincere and true. I have a great example to support this.

Svetlana was a member of my VIP program (she paid me to find the right man for her). She was a successful business owner of a real estate company in Kazakhstan and didn't place any emphasis on a man's income; she wanted to find someone who was kind, who loved children and would make a good role model for them, a real gentleman, of course, who would stand by her side and love her just the way she is.

Jim was a good, kind, giving middle-class man. The only problem was that he had lost nearly everything he had owned after his divorce with an American woman. I

introduced Svetlana to Jim via Skype; a month later the two met in the Dominican Republic – they connected the instant they saw each other.

Svetlana's attitude to Jim's situation was not something you would often find among American women: she was convinced that things would change after her arrival to the United States. And she was right. Once the two were married, Svetlana did all she could to improve their lives: she bought a house, started her own business, and helped her husband to get a huge promotion at work by believing in him, supporting him, and guiding him. Shortly after his promotion, Jim got an offer for a better job with a different company where he makes three times the amount he did before meeting Svetlana. This is a perfect illustration of the saying that there always is a wise woman behind every successful man. Oh, and did I mention that Svetlana is 5'9', has a body of a model and is 18 years younger than Jim?

Russian Russian vs. American Russian

It is also possible for you to meet a Russian woman who is already living in America, but you need to be aware of the fact that such women will be different from their fellow countrywomen. The table below lists qualities for both groups of women.

YOUR EXPECTATIONS FROM A WOMAN	Russian women in USA	Russian women abroad
She has to know English very well	60%	30%
Woman must relocate to my city or country (I live in a cold climate or state with 4 seasons)	Nearly 30% would agree; additional efforts on your part are required.	100% would agree.
She has to adapt her preferences to the lifestyle of a new country (food, music, reading, TV programs, friends).	Only 5% would agree.	60% of women would adjust their preferences to meet your expectations (this is accurate only for those women who don't have family and friends in the USA).

She has to be absolutely gorgeous, but be ready to meet an average guy with an average lifestyle.	10% chance.	100% chance.
She will be with a man 10+ years older than her.	30%	100%
A white female looking to meet a white male.	100%	100%
An Asian Russian looking to meet a white male.	20%	100%
A dark skin Russian looking to meet a white male.	2%	0.5%
A white female looking to meet an African-American man.*	15% - generally found in large cities.	60% in countries like Kazakhstan.
An Asian Russian looking to meet an African-American man.	20%	10% in countries like Kazakhstan.
A white female looking to meet an Asian man.	5%	15% in countries like Kazakhstan.
A woman prefers to travel to a man's country/home city for the first meeting.	10% chance.	80% chance.

COMMON STATEMENTS BY MEN	Positive response from Russian women in USA	Positive response from Russian women abroad
It is ok to check singles profiles even if I am married. I am not meeting anybody, so I am not hurting anybody.	10%	80%
I like to write about myself. The more I tell about myself via email, the higher chances of her being interested in me. I like to write at least 2 pages of bio.	5%	75%
I like to get to know people well via emails. I prefer to	0%	50%

correspond via email several times a week at least for 6 months before meeting in person.		
I sometimes smoke marijuana and occasionally use prescription drugs such as pain killers.*	10%	1%

YOUR HABITS	Positive response from Russian women in USA	Positive response from Russian women abroad
I have a moustache or a beard.	10%	50%
I live in the country and lead a simple life.*	5%	80%
I live in the country and lead an extravagant lifestyle; I want a girl who likes or wouldn't mind living in the country.	20%	90%
I live in a big city.	80%	100%
My education is less than a master's degree, but I have a clean job and a stable income.	90%	50%
I am a non-office worker (plumber, electrician, construction worker, handy man, etc.).	10%	80%
I am a government worker.	20%	100%
I like to talk on the phone for hours and prefer to get to know another person this way. We have to talk for several hours almost each day.	0%	80%
I want a woman who doesn't have kids and who doesn't want to have kids.	5%	1-5%

I want to get married and am mentally prepared to do whatever it takes when I meet the right woman.	100%	100%
I want to date someone for a year or more before deciding on engagement or marriage. I think living together is crucial in developing a relationship.	10%	20%
I am a free spirit, I travel, I enjoy life and don't worry much about what tomorrow brings. I don't care for money, I can live a very simple life, and there are always people who are willing to help me.	0%	0%
I definitely want to have children.	100%	100%
I think traditions are important.	100%	100%
I am an old school guy and a real gentleman.	100%	100%
I don't believe in spending money on spa visits, manicure, pedicure, stylist or designer shoes and clothes.*	* 5%	*15%

If you take a careful look at the listed percentages, you might find that in some cases response from women is not what you would expect. Let me give you a brief explanation of these.

Does race matter?

Ethnically, there are almost no black men in Russia, while Arabs and oriental men are more common. This makes mixed marriages rather rare and causes women to be unsure of what to expect; this means you might have to search a bit harder to find a woman who will not consider race an issue. In a nutshell, women from Central Asia countries (i.e. Kazakhstan) are more used to other ethnical groups as opposed to women from Russia or Ukraine. For example, 50% of the population in Kazakhstan looks oriental, so white Kazakh women would easily consider dating an oriental American and seem rather open to having a husband of different ethnic roots. Also, younger women are generally more flexible in the matter of skin color and are more willing to make daring steps. Women after 25 are usually more conservative in such matters. Relationship with your future bride's parents is also something to consider: while the older generation of Russians might not be racist, many older people are opposed to mixed marriages. If you have found a Russian woman willing to marry a man of a different race, make sure you discuss her parents' reaction to this as well to avoid conflicts in future.

But is it possible to find a Russian bride with model looks if you are an African American? Of course it is. Take a look at David and Alexandra. Alexandra, who certainly looks like a model, is originally from Kazakhstan. In fact, she used to work with models being a professional make-up artist, and while she prefers to make others beautiful rather than posing in front of the camera herself, she performed as a model several times as well. Oh, and David is 16 years older than Alexandra, but it doesn't bother her a bit.

If you look at Russian women who are already living in the United States, you will find that they are more open towards mixed marriages. While it is still a challenge to find someone who wants to marry an African-American or an Asian man, you might have a chance with women from large cities such as Los Angeles where such occurrences are more common.

Does location matter?

Are Russian women willing to live anywhere? Most Russian women prefer living in cities as opposed to rural areas. It has been a tendency in the US to move away from big cities to smaller towns and suburb areas; however, to most Russian women living away from the city means being stuck in the middle of nowhere and feeling isolated. This is largely due to their perception of how Russian villages and suburbs are: such areas are very remote and difficult to get to and live in.

If you live in a suburb area and are communicating with a woman who has never been to America, you will need to clarify that she would not be living in the wilderness. Explain to your Russian lady what is available close to where you live (stores, restaurants, etc.); make her understand that having a vehicle makes it convenient to travel wherever she needs (most people in Russia do not own cars and view them as luxury instead of necessity) and describe to her what accommodations your living quarters have (internet, phone, commodities, amenities, etc.). In other words, make her understand that she will be living in a civilized place, not in a wooden house without running water as can sometimes happen in Russian villages. Better yet, send her photos or a video of your home to avoid misunderstandings.

Still, sometimes the matter can simply lie in individual preferences: women who grew up in the city may simply not be willing to change the lifestyle they are used to. Women after 45-48 years of age are generally more willing to relocate in the countryside. The best way to truly understand your woman's likings, as with most cases, is to ask.

In fact, this book has a separate chapter on communicating with women to help you deal with such matters.

Many Russian women who live in the USA tend to move to large cities (Los Angeles, New York, San Francisco, etc.). Keep in mind that most women from Russia who are visiting America on a tourist visa come from large cities. You will notice that these women are far more advanced in their skills, careers, and financial stability. Generally they would not be willing to give up big city opportunities, although exceptions are possible.

Most women from large cities like Moscow visit America dreaming to meet a Hollywood actor or a multi-millionaire who would fall in love and want to marry her the second he sees her and finds out that she is from Russia. Blame Hollywood for the stereotypes – most women have seen "Pretty woman". So, in the beginning of their visit these women look for a Hollywood actor, a multi-millionaire, or, better, for a Hollywood actor who is a multi-millionaire. These hopes generally fade away fairly quickly, especially if they date some real life so-called producers or actors. Once these women have been in the US for 5-10 months, they generally realize that they want to meet a regular man to create a real family instead of chasing Hollywood ghosts. Why am I telling you this? If you prefer to meet Russian women who are already in the USA, select from women who have spent some time in the country.

Keep in mind that Russian women who have lived in America for 3 years or more would have undergone all possible changes in views and character and will probably be nothing like women who live in Russia. Such women would most likely have faced all sorts of troubles: getting settled, studying, learning the language, working several jobs to pay for the education, etc. These experiences will make them tough – America does not make life for foreigners easy (being a foreigner, I know). Such women will not settle for a man who has achieved less in life than they have. They will normally look for a man with good income, close in age and who is serious about a relationship. Such women will be blunt and straightforward. If they live in a large city, they are unlikely to want to relocate to a small town.

Whatever the case, if you want your Russian woman to relocate to a small town, you will have to communicate to her correctly (hint: the next chapter is all about communication!).

Do bad habits matter?

There isn't a definite answer as such preferences are usually strictly individual. However, drinking is an extremely common problem in Russia and some CIS countries, so you are more likely to get a negative reaction to this habit even compared to smoking. If you mention that you drink, explain how frequent/intensive your habit is: a few social drinks once in a while, a beer every evening, etc. Do not hide this information, as it will hurt your relationship in the long run, and if you are not willing to change your habit, certainly do not suggest otherwise.

Smoking is less likely to cause a negative reaction as many people in former USSR smoke, including women. In the recent years, the rate of smoking among women has increased drastically.

While in some states smoking marijuana is almost legal and is not heavily pursued by the law, to Russian women, especially those living abroad, marijuana is a very serious drug. If you hide the fact that you are a marijuana smoker, and your woman discovers this when she comes to United States, your relationships will most likely end up in divorce. You have to be upfront with your woman about taking any prescription drugs as well – you might get in trouble with her if you don't.

Whatever your habits, make sure that you include this information in your profile and/or mention it early on in your correspondence. Do not be afraid that some women might not accept your habits – there is a partner for everyone in this world, and the story below illustrates it well.

I had a female client, who was a gorgeous model in demand – she did photo shoots for many major fashion magazines, including cover for Vogue. She was a kind and a

giving girl... as long as she didn't drink – and that she did a lot (I am sure, you've heard what model lifestyle is like).

When she was drunk (which was about 70% of the time), she would cry on my shoulder asking why no one loved her. But when she was drunk, she was also very aggressive to men – being beautiful is not easy, she was often taken advantage or and learned to be defensive.

While she is not the type of woman I normally introduce my clients to, if you want a hot woman who will be fine with your bad habits, she would definitely be a potential match. Hey, not all Russian are angels – and I've never said they were!

On a serious note, you have to be honest about who you are if you want to attract the right woman into your life. Honesty goes a long way, and communication is the only key to solving any issues.

Do I really need to pay for spa treatments, designer shoes & clothes, manicure & pedicure?

Many men from abroad look for a beautiful Russian woman as their life partner and wife – isn't this why you are reading this book? Beautiful Russian women won hearts of many men from overseas, but very few men understand what it takes for a woman to maintain natural beauty and stunning appearance. It doesn't happen by itself and requires much effort and devotion on a regular basis.

I am sure you've seen a makeover show at least once in your life. A woman wearing a pair of jeans, an old t-shirt, and no makeup becomes a stunning beauty when she changes into a dress, a pair of heels, and has her hair/make up done. Give her an opportunity to attend a beauty salon, groom herself regularly, and have an expert work with her hair, face, and body, and you will always see a beautiful lady. On the other hand, leave her no chance for such activities, and very soon she will become an ordinary woman of average appearance.

Russian women are known for taking good care of their bodies and appearance. Most women you see on the streets are fit, dressed with taste, have their hair, makeup, and nails done at all times. Of course, you don't know how much time and money they put into manicure, pedicure, hairdresser, and spa activities, but when she comes to live in your country, she will be your responsibility – you will have a chance to find out the details and the cost of such activities soon enough. Your Russian bride will fully depend on you in your country because she will not be able to earn money as she did at home (at least, in the beginning of her stay). The same might be true if you marry a Russian woman who lives in the USA, especially if she has to relocate to be with you.

If you want your beautiful Russian wife to remain as beautiful as when you met her, you must be ready to pay for all the "girly" things that help her achieve this. Russian women stay fit because they do a lot of walking throughout the day just to get from one place to another. This will most likely change when she moves to your country which means she will need to go to the gym or at least have an option to exercise at home. Russian women dress well – skirts, dresses, suits, shoes, etc. If this is how you like to see her, don't expect to save money by shopping for jeans, t-shirts, and tennis shoes – this will make her just like every other woman around you. And, of course, doing nails, hair, and make-up goes without saying.

It seems almost cynical to talk about money when discussing beauty, but it is a part of life. And just because you will have to spend this money, it doesn't mean you will have to spend thousands of dollars every month. Besides, Russian women are good with money, so discuss these issues with your bride well in advance. Find out what she needs, what she expects, share your expectations with her, let her know what her budget will be, help her find the best way to manage this money, and so on. Russian men are very aware of beauty expenses for their women; they invest into their women's beauty without women having to bring up the matter. If you learn to do the same when dating a Russian woman, you will reap many rewards – your bride's beautiful appearance, good mood, and gratitude for your generosity.

If you think that paying for spa treatments, beauty salons, and fitness centers is foolish, then don't expect your Russian wife's appearance to remain the same as when you met her once she has lived in your country for a while. I know many Russian girls who moved abroad and changed their style to jeans and t-shirts, forgot about makeup and heels, and became just like other foreign women – it hasn't made them any worse as a person or a wife, but it made them plain average. If you are ok with that, you can ignore everything you have just read.

CHAPTER 3: ALL ABOUT YOU

What Russian women want

You might be ready to handle challenges of international dating and be perfectly organized to begin your search, but are you sure you are the kind of man who can appeal to Russian women? Take a look at the list below to find out if you have the qualities Russian women appreciate and look for in a partner.

1) A reliable man.
Russian women have a lot of responsibility in their lives, so to them finding a man who can take some of that responsibility off their shoulders is like finding a treasure. A reliable man is the one who is always near, psychologically speaking. He never expects the woman to take charge in solving problems or organizing the big things in life. He plans the first date to a tee, knowing where to go and what to do. His "yes" is "yes", his "no" is "no"; if he makes a promise, he keeps it. If a woman asks him to do something, she doesn't have to ask him again.

2) An attentive man.
Such a man knows what call of duty is. He readily cares for his wife and her family, grasping this duty calmly as something matter-of-course. He does so not because he has affection for these people, but because of his good attitude to his beloved woman.

3) A generous man.
Russian women see generosity as more than an unlimited credit account. To them, generosity of the heart is as important as generosity of the wallet. A generous man in their understanding is someone who protects weak and defenseless, offers help eagerly and doesn't expect to be rewarded in return.

4) A protector.
Russian women look for a man who will never expose his wife and his family to risk, even with regard to minor issues. Such a man

will never let his woman walk back home through the dark streets and will wait for her at the bus-stop if she is returning home late in the evening. A protector will never provoke conflict and will generally look for reconciliation and compromise.

5)   A faithful man.
A woman can forgive many flaws of a man if she is certain of his faithfulness. A faithful man doesn't need anyone except for his woman; he makes it clear to his partner and gives her no reason to question his integrity and faithfulness.

6)   A man who loves children.
Women with children are not the best "marriage material" in Russia. Often Russian men don't want to take care of their own children, much less someone else's. If you are dating a Russian woman with children, it is important that you convince her of your genuine interest and desire to care for her children after you are married – in this case, your woman's gratitude and affection will be without boundaries. Even if you are dating a woman who doesn't have children, she will most likely want to have kids. Your willingness to have children in future will certainly make you even more appealing to most women as very few of them will not want children.

7)   A man who doesn't think it's a shame to be divorced.
Many divorced women in Russia take care of their children; according to the latest sociological studies such women have little chance of marrying again. A part of it is the mentality of Russian men – they look for younger women without any "luggage". Divorced women are also quite limited in their choice: mortality rate of middle age males is very high.

8)   A man who is not afraid of responsibility and is willing to help out.
Most women in Russia have a peculiar lifestyle: they are generally overloaded with family responsibilities (housekeeping, taking care of parents, raising children) and have to work as well. Even though Russian men are often portrayed as rough and tough, you will find that men in Russia are not very helpful in terms of practical

matters; women generally take charge, solve everyday problems and manage essentials for the family.

9) A man who doesn't drink or drinks responsibly.
While not every Russian man is a drunk, consumption of alcohol is very high. This means that men prefer to spend money on alcohol instead of family needs, they can often be irresponsible and abusive. To put it briefly: Russian women are sick and tired to deal with the problem.

10) A man with a degree.
Most Russian women are educated. Since they often have to make a living, you will find many of them working in various fields, including law, education, and medicine which means they have to have a university degree. Most women don't care about the level of education their husband has, but they do care about being able to have an intelligent discussion.

11) A man with an entrepreneurial mind (a business man, a man capable of making sound decisions fast, a man who takes action).
Every year more and more Russian women become independent entrepreneurs, take lead positions in management, and start their businesses. When such a woman moves to a foreign country, she will want to have by her side a man who will help her establish herself as a business person. Note: Russian women prefer to become involved in business instead of building a corporate career; despite her interests, she will never choose her career over her man.

12) A man who encourages education for children.
As you already know, most Russian women have a university degree. Because education is important to them, Russian women want to have an opportunity to give their children quality education as well.

13) A man who values traditions.
Russian women are very a traditional, they respect older people, they know their role in the family, they expect their man to be a

provider, they know how to be a housewife, an excellent cook, and a wonderful wife to her husband, how to keep the house clean, and will respect their man. Even women-entrepreneurs or those with a career will maintain traditional values.

14) A man who respects other cultures.

Since you will be in a relationship with a foreign woman, it is important for you to respect her roots and where she came from. It doesn't mean that you have to love what she cooks, reads or listens to, but you need to be considerate of her choices and avoid criticism. Try to open your mind to new possibilities and new experiences.

15) A patient man who can compromise.

Because you are in a relationship with a woman of a different culture and mentality, you will have plenty of opportunities to exercise patience and tolerance. Your woman will be plunged into a new country with different traditions and mentality, and it will be up to you to make her feel comfortable in the new environment. Because Russian women are very traditional, you will also need to show your ability to compromise in adjusting the two cultures.

The background of Russian women is the reason marriages between American men and Russian women become successful – this is also supported by the latest studies. Practical stability of American men and family values of Russian women help create long-term alliances thanks to the clear distribution of family roles. Many American men have compared Russian women with a breath of fresh air – this becomes only more evident in comparison with career focused American women.

What about Russians, or why American men are a better fit for beautiful girls from Russia

If you wonder why Russian men are selfish, unfaithful, alcoholics, and wife beaters, it is because Russian women made them this way. Because the ratio of men to women is about 1:4 (in some regions it is 1:7!), women have to work hard to keep a man by their side as there always will be another woman who will be ready to please him more. Since Russian women know that it is potentially difficult to find a good man (yes, there are some, but they are far and few between!), they hold on to men in their lives by putting up with many things they don't like. Naturally, faithfulness is not a high priority for Russian men – they know they can easily find another woman to take care of all their needs.

------------------------------- Resource! --------------------------------
The explanation of the unbelievable tolerance from Russian women is disclosed in my free video series "The Path to the Russian Heart". You can get instant access to the series right after registering your free profile at www.OksanaLove.com/gift.

Still, it is very difficult for Russian women to find a decent man. This is where American men come in. Because most Americans are active, decisive, and can handle responsibility (something that most Russian men can't do), they are very attractive to Russian women - statistically, American men are among top sought after bachelors on Russian women's list.

Below is a table where I compare Russian and American men. Aside from satisfying curiosity, I want this table to become a brief study guide for you: as you look for a Russian wife, I suggest you take time to evaluate your personal qualities and make necessary changes or make the most of the qualities you possess that would appeal to a Russian woman.

- Statistics are based on my experience and men that join dating services.
- Highlighted are the boxed with qualities that women like.
- Explanation of points with asterisk is listed under the table.

TRAITS	RUSSIAN MEN	AMERICAN MEN	NEED TO LEARN FROM RUSSIAN MEN?
Drinking	Yes (a lot)	Sometimes	No
Education	Yes	Sometimes	Yes
Smoking	Very often	Often	No
Faithfulness	Very uncommon	Almost always	No
Younger appearance	No	Yes	No
Healthier life style	No	Yes	No
Chivalrous	Yes	Uncommon (10%)	Yes
Poor personal hygiene	Yes	No	Hell, NO!
Sexual health and fitness maintained even after 50	No	Yes	No
Expect a woman to tidy their personal affairs or financial issues	Yes	Very uncommon	No
Help around the house with chores	Very uncommon	Yes	No
Cheating	Very common	Very seldom	NO, NO, NO!
Take care of their children even when divorced	Very uncommon	Very common	No
Cautious about getting women pregnant*	No	Yes	No
Always bears financial responsibility*	Yes	Uncommon	Yes/No
Speak their mind *	Yes	No	Yes
Demanding and in charge in sexual matters*	Yes	Uncommon	Yes/No
Remains involved in raising children	Very uncommon	Very common	No
Flashy, love to show off*	Yes	No	Yes/No

Will defend and protect under any circumstances	Yes	Not often	Yes

Always bears financial responsibility – a small correction: Russian men always bear financial responsibility when they are in love. They never question who will pay for a date (it is nonsense to go Dutch); they will definitely pay for a vacation if it is to be shared with his woman even if the two are not married; they will certainly pay for woman's shopping, spa, etc. However, when they decide to move on to the next woman, it is highly unlikely for them to continue to support former partners financially. The latter attitude is not something to follow, but it is a good idea to take on the attitude of a Russian man in love.

Cautious about getting women pregnant – Russian men believe that it is a woman's responsibility to be careful when it comes to getting pregnant; men don't believe they have to stay around or participate in the upbringing of children if a woman becomes pregnant.

Speak their mind – American men are often afraid of hurting people's feelings so they try to be diplomatic, but it is not always the best way to communicate with Russian women. Culturally, Russians are rather blunt; if you are not clear in your opinions or statements, there is much room for interpretation (*read*: misunderstanding).

Demanding and in charge in sexual matters – American men are more mindful of women's wants and desires, but it isn't always a good thing. Russian women like when a man takes the first step and shows initiative (a good thing about Russian men), but they like to be treated with respect and consideration once the relationship progresses (something Russian men lack).

Flashy, love to show off – Russian men are known for their bravado, they are like peacocks with their tails spread out. However, most of it happens when they are drunk. Russian women like some of such attitude – in their mind it is a sign of "manliness", but you don't want to overdo it as it will have a reverse effect.

Myths Russian women have about foreign men

Many Americans think Russia doesn't have running water and that bears walk on the streets of Russian cities. But stereotypes go both ways, and there are some myths circulating about foreigners as well. When you hear them, you might get a better idea as to why Russian women react a certain way to foreign men.

Myth 1 - Foreigners are stupid.

One of the main causes for this is... Hollywood. Many American films and shows that have reached Russia are full of slapstick humour which is not really accepted by Russians. The result: Russians think that Americans laugh at stupid things. Some Russian comics have taken full advantage of this and have contributed by further inflating this idea through making fun of American culture (i.e. strange laws, habits, etc.).

Myth 2 – Foreigners always smile, even without any reason.

You will not see many smiling people on the streets of Russia, and it isn't because Russians don't like to or don't know how to have fun. Most people in Russia think a person must have a good reason to smile, unless he or she is up to something or is making fun of somebody. It is very much a cultural thing – there is a time and a place for smiling and having fun, it is not something that happens commonly.

Another reason for such attitude is that ongoing challenges of life have also left a definite imprint on people's attitudes – when a person is constantly occupied by trying to find ways to make both ends meet, he/she is not very likely to look at the brighter side of things.

Myth 3 – Americans are arrogant and cocky.

Unfortunately, many visitors from the US were the ones that created this stereotype. Many American visitors have often harshly criticized the way things are in Russia and have made loud claims that the United States is the only nation that has it right. Russians are very sensitive when it comes to criticism of their home: they know very well it is a mess, but it is theirs, and no one from abroad has room to criticize. As a result, Russian people have grown to resent Americans for such attitude and often transfer this stereotype on every visitor from the US, even if the person does not share such views.

Of course, things you find in Russia may often seem unusual or even strange to you, but the best thing you can do is ask about it and smile politely. Under no circumstances you should compare it to the way it is done in your country and claim that your people have the right solution, as this will most likely offend your hosts or native friends.

Myth 4 – If a man is using an online dating service to look for a wife (especially if he has never been married), there has to be something wrong with him.

Of course, there is little logic behind such thinking since thousands of Russian women are using the same services to look for a husband abroad, but, on the other hand, it is completely justified as Russian women know there is nothing wrong with them, but who knows about those foreigners? After all, many men from overseas wonder the same thing – why is it that beautiful, smart women look for partners outside of their home country? Negative publicity has significantly contributed to women fearing that a guy from a dating service will turn out to be a maniac or someone looking for a housekeeper or a babysitter for his children.

When you are corresponding with Russian women, be frank in explaining why you are still single, find a tactful way to mention that there is nothing physically or mentally wrong with you, and do not bring up sex or intimate subjects until you and your lady are comfortable with your relationship.

Myth 5 – Living abroad is a fairy tale; foreign men are stable, honest, generous, and kind.

While this idea has been slightly tarnished by select negative stories, Russian women still believe that living abroad will be a step above their life in Russia and that foreign men appreciate women more than men at home. However, do not think that Russian women expect something extraordinary from men – they simply want a normal relationship. They want for their mate to have good education and stable employment, they want him to take care of his family, to be attentive, and not be a drunkard.

Now, when you communicate with someone from Russia, you will know why people react funny when you smile at them or why they are shocked you haven't been married by the age of 30. If you explain why you are the way you are, how things work in your country, and what you think/feel, you will avoid being labeled a "typical" foreigner and will be able to have a much better relationship with a Russian woman.

Russian woman will never be yours, if...

By now you know that a Russian woman is perfect for any man, but if you think that any man with a foreign passport is perfect for a Russian woman, think again. While a Russian woman will always stand by her man and can forgive many things, some categories of men will never appeal to her.

Group 1. Arrogant men thinking that any woman would jump into their arms when they flash an American passport. What a huge mistake to think so! I've lost count of how many men were told off, wasted money and, most importantly, never found a decent bride because of having this attitude.

Group 2. Close-minded men. Marrying a foreign woman means that you have to be open-minded – you can't expect your Russian wife to isolate herself from her previous life, roots, culture, and traditions. I know many American men who demanded that their Russian wives stop listening to Russian songs, stop eating and cooking Russian food, and stop talking Russian to their friends. Seriously?! Russian women will change and adapt to American culture, but it will not happen overnight; and they will never give up their heritage, period.

Group 3. Messy men. There is nothing wrong with keeping your

high-school memorabilia or your drawings from primary school, but if this stuff is piled up in your garage among dirty pizza boxes, you've got a problem (and not just from Russian women's point of view). Russian women are very neat; they are excellent housewives, who keep clean, organized houses. If your house looks like a hurricane went through it when your woman comes

to live with you, she is not going to be very happy. She will not make a scene, but she will clean and re-arrange everything. Don't try to stop her, instead try to support her. If you are not ready for it, be prepared for a relationship disaster as your lady will not tolerate it for long.

Group 4. Overweight + sloppy + lazy + couch potato. I don't mean

to offend anyone, but this issues has to be addressed. I understand that obesity can sometimes be a result of serious hormonal problems, but this is not what I am talking about. I am referring to eating-pizza-and-fast-food-all-day-long-followed-by-containers-of-beer type of obesity.

You picked up this book because you want to find a beautiful girl. It is only fair that a beautiful woman would want to see by her side a presentable, clean man who takes care of his health. After all, it requires a lot of work for any girl to stay beautiful and fit for her man, so why can she not expect that her man would want to do the same for her? If you were a beautiful woman, would you want to date a guy in the photo? No one would ever believe you if you said "yes"! Appearances don't really matter to Russian women, but there is a certain level of self-respect that will keep any woman from being with a man so extremely neglected.

LESS EXTREME GROUPS:

Group 5. Men who don't want to have children. As Russian women are generally very traditional, they almost always want to have children when creating a family. If you have children of your own and don't plan to have more, but want to marry a young woman, you should seriously reconsider your position or look for a woman in her 40's who has had children already and will not mind your choice.

Group 6. Hairy Harry. This is not a joke. Russian women do not like moustache and beards. They are sensitive, with very gentle skin, and don't like kissing a man with hair on his face. They are not into long hair either – to them, long hair is a privilege of a woman and not something men should have. What they like is a classic European clean-cut look.

Group 7. Men who wear bad cologne. Again, this is not a joke. Russian men often don't smell very good because they don't shower often, but they have figured out how to use fragrances. Russian women are very sensitive to smells, so the way you smell is important – if you don't smell good, you won't be attractive.

Give preference to smells like "Chanel Egoiste" or "Givenchi Blue" – these smells are sexy, business-man like, and very charming. If you tend to use "sweet" fragrances, get rid of them once and for all when meeting Russian women – such smells remind them of their grandfather's colognes (they are even called "grandpa" fragrances).

Group 8. Men who dress badly. Russian women can tolerate many things, but they definitely aren't fond of the "comfortable American style" – especially when it comes to favourite jeans and t-shirts, wrinkled and with holes. The best option is to wear a clean ironed shirt and slacks (maybe jeans) – it might seem like a small thing, but it helps to create a good impression. Once again, if you are looking for a beautiful woman who pampers and grooms herself to make you proud when you walk next to her, it is only fair that you do the same.

CHAPTER 4: A PERFECT START

Long before dating a Russian woman

You are certainly familiar with the term "the power of thought" – if you visualize something clearly, persistently, and long enough, your dream will come true. While I believe in this concept, it often acts as

a stumbling block for men in their search – they become content with thinking and forget to act. If you truly want to find a gorgeous, smart woman as your partner, you need to be active, and you can easily achieve this goal in 90 days.

As with any other goal, you first need to decide on an acceptable timeframe. Instead of saying that you might meet your perfect woman someday, you need to set a specific date – after all, YOU are driving the process and making the decision as to when you want to meet her. This simple change will set your mind into an active mode, thus making your search more successful.

Let me draw a parallel with finances. If you know when you will receive your paycheck, you can plan your expenses. You can decide exactly how much you want spend and know what you can and cannot afford – in other words, you can create a clear mental picture of what things will be like from paycheck to paycheck. If your paycheck doesn't come regularly, or you receive a check for a different amount every time, you will have no idea as to what you will be able to afford until you have it in your hand, making it impossible to plan and organize your life.

The same is true for your personal life – if you plan to meet your partner some day in the future, your mind is not looking for favourable opportunities, and you are not ready for action. So, if you wonder why you are still single and haven't met that perfect woman, it is probably because you don't have a plan.

Truth is, your life is full of beautiful women ready for a relationship; every day you pass them on the streets, sit next to them in a restaurant or meet them at your workplace. So why aren't you in a relationship with any of them? The answer is simple – because you are not giving off the right vibes. I am not talking about some voodoo mumbo-jumbo, I am talking about basic psychology – when you are ready to meet someone, consciously and subconsciously you send out signals that tell the opposite sex about your intentions. If you think you'd like a relationship, but are not ready for one, you send those signals too! What's even worse, when you are looking for a relationship without being mentally prepared for it, you end up attracting the wrong kind of women – women that are not your type, women you don't feel comfortable with, and women who have nothing in common with your dream woman.

So, how do you create a dating plan? These simple steps will give you a good start.

Create a "dating Calendar"

Where do you find one? Since you purchased this book, you can get a free calendar at OksanaLove.com.

After you register your profile, I will mail you a calendar with photos of our 12 most attractive single women who are actively looking for a husband. I know every one of them personally and think that seeing their beautiful faces and smiles is the best incentive you can have to encourage you in your 90-day search.

Aside from being full of beautiful photos of single women you can meet, the calendar has a very important function – it will help you organize your search and map out its most important landmarks.

Before you start filling out the calendar, you must consider a few things. The first important thing to consider is the location of your dream woman – does she live in your country or are you looking for a Russian bride overseas? This is a crucial factor which will determine how much time you have for all other activities. For example, if you want to meet a woman that lives overseas, you have to allow at least 2-3 months for communication and planning the trip. Even if you want to be with a woman who lives in the same country as you, there might still be plenty of things to prepare before the meeting takes place – you might need to get your house in order for your future wife to see the way you live, to improve your wardrobe and grooming if need be, to sort out any unfinished personal business, etc. All these things are essential to make a good impression on a woman you like and to prove that you are ready for commitment and a serious relationship.

You might think that you can manage these things as your relationship progresses, but my experience shows that it never really works – there is nothing more permanent than a temporary solution. If you leave important things "for later", you risk to never get them done, thus robbing yourself of a chance to be with the right woman.

Create a master list

Now you need to make a list of everything you need to do to ensure a perfect meeting with the perfect woman. This list needs to include everything that you need to do up to the moment you meet her, from writing down the description of your future Russian wife and planning your budget for travel to losing weight and shopping for clothes.

If you think this is an unnecessary step, let me assure you that it is not so. Once you embark on your search, things can get overwhelming really fast – remember, you are on a 90-day deadline! If you have the list of all the activities in front of you, you can plan and schedule them at a comfortable pace, focusing on all the right things. Otherwise, it is easy to get distracted or miss something, so by the time your perfect woman will be ready to meet you, you will not be ready to meet her.

Block and mark all tasks

Now that you have a master list of everything you need to do to create a great impression on your Russian woman, you need to create time blocks and mark all deadlines in the calendar. If you have allowed yourself four weeks to get in shape by going to the gym three times a week, mark that on the calendar. If you know that you need to plan a shopping trip within the next month, select a day for it and stick to the chosen date. Once you complete this part of your preparation, make sure you look at your calendar daily and mark the progress of your preparation. For example, if you are trying to lose weight, mark your progress every day; if you have completed a visit to the travel agency, cross it off on the calendar.

Now, the final point: don't delay, create the calendar right now (well, maybe after you finish reading the book, or at least this chapter!). The sooner you organize your thoughts about all the things you need to do, the sooner you will be truly ready to meet a wonderful Russian woman with confidence and ease.

-------------------------------- Resource! --------------------------------
To receive your free copy of "The Most Beautiful Russian Women In the World" wall calendar + IN-DEPTH background of each of the ladies presented in it, visit *www.OksanaLove.com/gift* to register your profile, use **FREE416** in the promo code field to claim your complimentary gift.

Ready, set, dream

Truth be told, not every man who comes to my agency finds the woman of his dreams... simply because most men have NO clue what their perfect woman is. They have a fairly vague picture in their mind of what they want – young, beautiful, sexy, but that is just a tip of the iceberg.

To really know what your perfect woman is like, you need to think about everything she is: appearance, family situation, age, personal qualities, and so on. But you also need to know what it is that you want – what qualities attract you to women, what you can tolerate, and what you absolutely cannot stand in a partner.

I cannot stress enough how important it is for you to determine what you want in a woman. Otherwise, you will spend months (and hundreds of dollars if you decide to meet) on every "young, beautiful, sexy" girl on the dating websites you visit (there are hundreds of them out there!) without accomplishing anything. I suggest a few simple exercises to help you get your thoughts in order.

First, write down all the details about the woman you want to have in your life, just like you did with your dating calendar. And your description has to go beyond "Oh, as long as she is not a smoker", because in THIS case why not enjoy yourself with a fat, ugly, retired alcoholic? So long as she is not a smoker, of course. You have to be specific and you have to write it down, because that is the best way to sort all your thoughts. The tables below will help you with this task – they contain suggestions of things to consider, but feel free to add and expand the list.

My strong suggestion is to avoid making any comparison with celebrities. Don't ask for your perfect woman to look like Angelina Jolie, for example. The actress changes from film to film – a blonde, a brunette, a rebellious teenager or a seductive siren, so it is impossible to create a clear picture in your mind of what you want. Besides, what happens if tomorrow you decide that you favour Halle Berry instead – will you want for your woman to change? If you absolutely must refer to a celebrity, record qualities or specific features you like.

APPEARANCE *(include features that are important to you such as height, weight, eye color, hair color, body type, age.)*

LIFESTYLE *(include features that are important to you such as country of residency, family status, children, spoken languages, education level, occupational status.)*

PERSONALITY *(include traits that are important to you – kindness, being athletic, sense of humour, religious preferences, common interests. It is beneficial to reflect upon your past relationships to determine what you liked and didn't like.)*

QUALITIES I WILL NOT TOLERATE *(include traits that you are not prepared to tolerate in a partner – be honest, as your future depends on this. Again, it is beneficial to look back at your past relationships and evaluate things that went wrong, that turned you off, that didn't work and made you unhappy.)*

This exercise is A MUST for every gentleman searching for his ideal partner. Whether you believe it or not, our mind only works towards a specific goal when it has a clear picture of what the goal is. This is described in great detail in the documentary "The Secret" by Rhonda Byrne which explains how you can make your dreams come true through visualization and the power of thought. Feel free to put watching it on your to-do list in the dating calendar – valuable advice and mind training techniques from leading motivational and empowerment gurus will certainly help you in your search.

CHAPTER 5: MARKETING YOURSELF

Don't sell yourself cheap

I know it might sound a little odd, but looking for a quality relationship is almost the same as looking for a good job: you want both to be satisfying and to make you happy. When placing your information online, consider it a marketing task – you being the marketed item. In order to market a product well, you must first know it inside and out. This means, you might have to do a lot of self-digging: what are your best traits, values, unique abilities, and qualities? You must know well what makes you unlike everyone else. In a way, your profile is your resume – you must put your best foot forward in just a few lines. Avoid using generic phrases. This is no time for being shy – highlight your strong sides, describe your interests and inner world (without sounding boastful, of course!). It is not an easy task, so you will likely spend some time mulling over all the answers you want to include in your profile. And just as with your resume, a correctly filled out profile will attract only the best candidates.

While you are, in fact, selling and marketing yourself to women, unlike most of the annoying marketers and salesmen, you don't have thousands and hundreds of thousands of clients to pitch to. You only have a few, and you have to make each one of them count.

It all starts with creating your best online presentation.

In the previous chapter you read about the type of men Russian women are attracted to. I know from personal experience that Russian women go absolutely crazy about men in suites; even a dress shirt with a tie has all chances of getting their attention. The reason is simple - such outfit creates an image of a successful man that Russian women cannot resist; to them it means authority, credibility, and respect – exactly what they are attracted to.

It goes without saying that the style and the fit of your suit should be impeccable, it has to be clean and ironed. If you are not very good at choosing clothes and matching colors, visit a shopping mall and ask for assistance from an experienced sales person (bringing along an honest friend is a bonus). Don't forget about the shoes – make sure they complete your overall image and are polished. An impeccable outfit that speaks "confidence" must appear in your photos, it is what you should be wearing when you meet your woman for the first time, either via video or in person.

Working on your appearance must begin long before you plan a meeting with the woman of your dreams. A photograph is an essential part of your profile, and I am going to tell you how to create an outstanding photo collection to get maximum hits and responses to your profile.

Naturally, photograph is what attracts a person's attention to a profile when he/she is browsing though hundreds or thousands of personal ads. People are more likely to open profiles that contain photographs. This means you only have one chance to grab a woman's attention and get her to read what you have to say about yourself.

Ask a friend to take your photos – an iPhone or any smartphone has a good enough camera to take adequate photos. But if you want a killer shot, use services of a professional photographer. You don't have to go for hundreds of photos – a few various poses and expressions will do. And whatever you do, do not take photos of your reflection in a mirror – they will not create the impression you are looking for!

 Russian women like clean photos – they like well-dressed men, who are clean and neat. This is exactly what your photos should look like, regardless of your line of work. If you are a construction worker and submit a photo of yourself in your work clothes, don't be surprised if you don't attract women's attention. Instead, dig through your closet, get out your suit (a pair of slacks, a dress shirt and a tie will also do) and

get yourself together for a few shots (yes, even if you do not feel comfortable wearing such an attire!). The photo on the left is a great example.

If you are not convinced, maybe this story will change your mind. I once had a private client (he is happily married now) who is a great man: simple, easy to get along with, very kind and considerate, with a great sense of humour, but of average appearance – just your ordinary guy. He was a farmer and enjoyed his work a lot. He was so proud of his occupation that he wanted to share all the glory of it with the Russian women on the dating website – he included in his profile photos of himself using machinery and driving a combine harvester (even though he rarely drives it and generally only manages harvesting). Guess what the response rate from women was? About 10%.

When he asked me for help, it didn't take me long to explain to him how he has misrepresented himself in the photos: while he gets out in the field from time to time, most of his work is in the office (managing, controlling, contracting, conducting meetings, and so on). Looking at his photos, women thought he spends all of his time slaving away in the dirt and has no life outside the field, although he spends half his time in a condo on a beach near Florida, is a frequent traveler, and loves the Caribbean.

The first change I made was to his online image to reflect his life the way it really is. Yes, I made him wear one of his suites for the photos as well as told him to post photos of his condo and photographs from his travels. He also added photos of his house. His response rate went to almost 80%! Not bad, huh? With just these few changes almost every girl he contacted wanted to talk to him.

Getting back on the subject, what should you include in your collection of photos?

Work photos. It is beneficial to add some photos of your work or you at work – they will help women imagine all aspects of your life vividly. Photos in the office are quite a hit within Eastern European ladies. If you are a business man, use it as a photo opportunity. Most women are drawn to men of authority – show them you are the boss and you are guaranteed attention and numerous letters.

Your life. Showing details of your everyday life will help your woman imagine a life together. Show her your surroundings, so she can understand what her life will be when she moves in with you. This can be done by displaying photos of your house/apartment, your car, etc. Remember, Russian women keep clean and neat homes, so make sure everything is tidy and in place before taking photos.

A few words about car photos – most Russian women (the ones who live overseas) would not understand what a "truck" means; to her it can very well mean that you drive a semi-truck. Also, all SUV's and trucks in Russia are called a "jeep". So, it is better if you can add some photos to show her what you really mean.

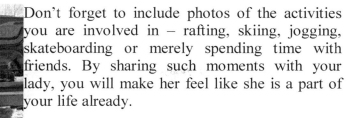

Don't forget to include photos of the activities you are involved in – rafting, skiing, jogging, skateboarding or merely spending time with friends. By sharing such moments with your lady, you will make her feel like she is a part of your life already.

Your children. If you have any children who live with you and who your future wife would need to help you to raise, I suggest you add their photos to your profile as well. This is important since a woman will become their step mother and she will certainly want to see those photos too. And what can be better than showing her your happy family with smiley cute little faces on these photos?

Your country, state, city. Men often don't think about posting such photos, but it is highly advisable. You can write volumes about how beautiful your country or city is, but a picture is truly worth a thousand words. Most women will not be able to imagine your living conditions (same as you will most likely not be able to imagine her living conditions and situation), unless they can see it. They might be able to find some information online, but since most women have limited Internet access and some of them might not know how to use a computer, it will be a lot easier for them to see photos in your profile. The same goes for women who live in the USA – you will be surprised, but the stats of my agency show that in many cases women from California have never visited any other state and have no idea what other cities/states look like.

Create a Unique Personal Proposition (UPP)

We've finally reached the next stage of your search, and you will need to take further action and complete another task. Make sure that you have completed homework from the first chapter (describing your ideal woman in detail), because we will be returning to the results of that step several times throughout this book and you will have to do it sooner or later if you really want to get results.

You already know that it is your task to sell yourself to women at the best price; that price is the most desirable woman who is the exact match to the list you have created (you see, you really should go back to chapter four and get it done!). If you want to sell yourself, you need to know how to market yourself – this means you need to tell women why they should choose you over the next guy... and before you can tell them why they should choose you, you need to understand why they would do that... and before you can understand why they would choose you, you need to know what women want.

You differentiate yourself from the competition by determining your best qualities (and, as an added bonus, this is an opportunity for you to feel better about yourself and boost your confidence a little if you are feeling uncertain about your ability to conquer any woman). Now, take a piece of paper and make another list that can answer any woman's question "Why should I choose you over any other man approaching me right now?"

Any woman should choose me over other men, because I am...
Caring
Financially stable
Have a good sense of humor
Giving
Understanding
Love to dance
Love to give massages

```
Love children
Great cook
Good with tools
Love to travel
…….
```

Again, go crazy with this list – include every little thing you can think of that makes you a wonderful guy, a treasure for any woman; talk to your friends and ask for their input – this is very helpful as other people generally can tell us many more things about ourselves we wouldn't think about.

Now you need to analyze this list. Look at all the qualities you wrote down and think how they would add value to a woman's life. This is probably the most intense portion of the entire process – you really need to step into a woman's shoes to realize what these qualities can mean to her as your partner. If you can determine how your personal qualities can change her life for the better, adding value to it, you can be certain that you will be able to attract her attention and make her fall in love with you.

Qualities from the list above	How would this quality improve my woman's life?
Caring	She will receive comfort and support.
Financially stable	She will feel secure; I can help her create or establish her business.
Loving children	I will make a great dad and role model for her child.
Business savvy	I can help her make her business successful.

Love to give massages	I will make her relax and remove her stress level after a busy work day.
Love to dance	A great chance to spend quality time together and avoid routine in personal life.
Handy person	The house is always in good shape, things are always fixed.

As you compose this list, you might find that some of your qualities are exactly what women are looking for, while others will make no difference to them. Knowing this, you need to highlight the qualities that can bring a positive change to a woman's life – that is how you can make sure that women become attracted to you and see your true colors. I suggest that you keep this list and refer to it from time to time, as it is something that will greatly benefit you in future at any stage of a relationship.

------------------------------ Resource! ------------------------------
Oksana Live TV show contains a couple of great videos where I talk about how you get yourself "identified as a catch". You can access these video episodes right after registering your profile at *www.OksanaLove.com/GIFT*

CHAPTER 6: COMMUNICATING WITH YOUR RUSSIAN BRIDE

Now that you have polished your online image, it is time to think about the way you will communicate with Russian women. I explain the basic principles of successful communication using emails as an example, but the same principles apply to every aspect of your communication, including video and face-to-face meetings.

-------------------------------- Resource! ----------------------------------
All examples and templates were taken from my program "MAGNETIC EMAIL: Your guide to effective written communication".

To get more information and access a free webinar go to www.OksanaLove.com/Gift. You will receive access to the webinar after a free registration of your profile.

Before you write your first email to a beautiful Russian woman, here is what you should remember if you want her to be interested in talking to you:

1. Be attentive.

This is your biggest key to really getting to know a woman who is of interest to you. Speaking, chatting, or communicating in person with a lady that makes your heart beat faster can be intimidating. It is easy to focus on finding the next best thing to say to impress her than to actually listen to what she is saying. But you should pay close attention to the information she is sharing and note down (mentally or physically) things she says. Build on what has already been said by asking related questions – this is the best way to find out who your lady of choice really is, what her goals are, and if she is the best match for you.

2. Be courteous and respectful.

Russian women are very giving; once they sense interest, they will put emotional value in your communication. It is important that you show her respect in return, make an effort to be a good listener, learn to sense when she is talking about things that are really important to her, and don't take these things lightly. Keep your conversations and language respectful; be certain that your lady is open to personal communication before you bring up any private topics, and remember that Russian women appreciate being treated like ladies.

3. Keep family in your discussions.

Russian women are known for their commitment to family and being family-oriented which makes them great wives and mothers. Family remains the center of their lives; asking your lady about it will give your sweetheart a chance to share things closest to her heart, while you will have a chance to discover some of the most personal things about her life and who she is. Do not hesitate to share with your lady information about your family as well – it will show her that you are taking your relationship seriously; your Russian beauty will appreciate your interest and ability to share special things. But… before you start discussing family, you must remain "an orphan" during you first 2-3 conversations (via email, phone or in person). Until then, do not bring family into conversation unless you are asked, and even when you are asked, keep your answer short and sweet.

4. Better ask than assume.

Mass media has painted many different portraits of women from Russia – poor, neglected, desperate to leave their home, waiting for foreigners to "save" them. But reality is often much more than that: many women are interested in finding a true partner to love and care for, someone who can be a great husband and father, someone to share their life with. You need to learn to see beyond stereotypes; better ask your lady about what things really are like instead of making false assumptions which can offend your sweetheart.

5. Don't forget your sense of humor.

Everyday life of people in Russia gives them little reason to smile, so your lady will appreciate you making her smile and laugh, especially if it comes naturally. Most Russian women are cultured and educated, so intelligent and sensible jokes will yield much better results than rough and crude humor. Make sure that you do not use humour that involves cartoon characters or movies that came out more than 10 years ago as your woman will not be able to relate to them. A good rule of thumb – use picture humor (for example, caricatures) which will be much easier for her to understand.

6. Honesty is the best policy.

Any woman will appreciate this quality in a man. Being honest with your lady will help you build trust and show her that you are reliable – something many Russian women do not find in men at their home country. It can be easy to "omit" or "change, just a little bit" some things about your life, but it is not a good idea as such "white lies" can ruin a great relationship later. Such topics as children, money, or your communication with other women (if it is the case) should in particular be discussed honestly at all times – your lady will appreciate the truth and you will be certain that you found the woman who likes you for who you really are.

7. Looks matter... or do they?

It is typical for men to think that Russian women are only interested in men who look like movie stars – a common mistake made because men are usually the ones looking for models. An average Russian woman will love you for who you are more than for what you look like, and women's preferences vary when it comes to appearance (same as they do for most men). When making an impression it is more important to show that you take time to take care of yourself and make a point to be well-groomed. This means finding clothes that fit your body best, a haircut that suits your face, not using potent smelling cologne or aftershave, etc. – things we've already discussed.

8. Be confident and have a goal.

Scammers have given Russian women a poor reputation of being interested only in money.

While some are, most women are not looking for a bank account. What they are interested in most is a steady life and your ability to take care of her and your future family. They want to be certain that a man can be a shoulder to lean on and someone who can provide a comfortable life. This does not mean you have to be a millionaire, but being confident of your goals and sharing them with your lady will send her the right message.

It is impossible to foresee everything that can go wrong in your email communication, but there are some things that are guaranteed to send women running. In the following few paragraphs, I outline the basic mistakes men make in emails. I will also provide some examples of letters that are full of mistakes and things you should avoid in your emails if you want a woman to write you back.

Generic letters

You must have received at least one sales or advertisement letter in your life. Do you remember what you felt reading it, holding it in your hands? An impersonal piece of paper, cloned for hundreds or thousands of people, signed by someone with no real face or, sometimes, even without a name. Sales people and marketers are annoying, their messages are boring. Unfortunately, many letters that end up in Russian women's inboxes look and feel the same – it is excusable, but completely unproductive.

Just for a minute, imagine receiving such a letter. How would it make you feel? It probably wouldn't really inspire you to write back. If that's so, why do you think it would make any woman want to reply? Sadly, such letters make up about 90% of all correspondence in my agency.

Talking too much about yourself

This is one of the biggest mistakes many men make. Now I want you to think for a minute about the most annoying and unattractive advertisement you've ever seen. It is probably one of those infomercials that sound something like this: "This is XYZ; it is fantastic because it does this and that. You need XYZ, because it is the best thing out there. Call us and buy XYZ now if you don't want to miss out. You haven't called us yet? This is your last chance to buy XYZ..." and so on. Annoying, aggravating, and makes you want to strangle someone. That's pretty much how women feel when they get letters that talk about you – well, only about you.

Naturally, when you are interested in a woman, you want to share everything about yourself with her, but there really can be too much of a good thing. Human beings absorb information in small portions – scientists suggest that at any given time we digest only about 10% of all information we receive. This means that any letter with excessive information about you and your life will read to a woman like this, "Hi, my name is John. I am 43, blah-blah-blah-blah-blah, I like dogs, blah-blah-blah-blah-blah. Occasionally I like to go fishing, blah-blah-blah-blah-blah." Is this what you really want?

If you really wish to grab a woman's attention and secure a response to your letter, you need to focus on the woman you are writing to and keep information about yourself to a bare minimum. It might be hard, but think of it as a necessary sacrifice to build a better future for your relationship. Once the two of you have connected and established mutual interest, you will have all the time in the world to tell her about your fishing trips and dental appointments.

Hello, Tatyana,

Seriously, you are more than attractive, I would say really hot. I would be happy to write to you more and learn about you, and if you are interested I am happy to tell you more about myself.

However, there is a problem. Correspondence can be exciting for a while, as new things are learnt, but eventually (and that should be sooner rather than later) a face-to-face meeting is essential. I explored previously the possibility of travelling to Kazakhstan. I must tell you it is not so easy, possibly one of the most difficult places in the world because of distances and visas. I have travelled through western Russia to St Petersburg and Moscow, so I know those great cities are more established for tourists. I know the scenery is magnificent but Kazakhstan is not the number one tourist place in the world.

My experience is that letters are a poor substitute for a meeting, for both the man and woman because photos can be old, people change and people's perception of themselves is not the same as reality sometimes.

I am sure you understand the truth in all of my explanation. So, before we embark on writing to each other we need to agree that a meeting is essential, in a country that we both feel comfortable. My atlas suggests that place would be Thailand, you wouldn't worry also about your safety there at least.

Briefly, about myself, I do not have a regular job at a company. I am my own boss and my own employee. I have sold my home and my life is contained in two suitcases and I have a laptop. I travel where I want to (so long as there is a good internet connection). I have created a life where I want to travel and see the world, but share that with someone whom I am in love with. I want to feel like a teenager and want to have my almost-twin to share all. I really enjoy conversation, intelligent discussion about all things, passions about life, food and ideas. I have not arrived at the present situation easily. I have planned for 3 years to create this possibility.

To help you further decide about me, you must feel a sense of adventure also, be very capable in all things, not fussy, easy going, adaptable, see wonder in simple things. One day such a life as I will lead will come to an end, and a house and less serendipity will ensue, but until then my plan is simple, the details are vague except what I have told you. To save further time, I will attach below a brief standard letter about my life. Of course, it needs to be standard because I have only one life :-)

I was born in England. My parents migrated to Australia when I was 6 months old. I lived a happy childhood in a city called Adelaide. I trained as a Chemical Engineer. I am not exact and think more like the scientist with his head in the clouds.I married in 1979. We went to USA in 1982 to work on military rockets. My oldest daughter was born in Alabama. I also learnt to fly a small airplane as a hobby. Two fun years in USA with plenty of travel and sightseeing.

My middle daughter and my son were born in Australia. The family moved to Brisbane in 1992. I worked as a farmer on my brother-in-law's large farm. The work was enjoyable seeing big fields of wheat grow. In one year, we grew 2500 tons of wheat. For two men this is a big effort. This period of my life was a great enjoyment and pleasure on the farm, but also of great difficulty because there was little money.

In 1996, my life changed again. I became an Executive (manager) in a large industrial company. I spent one year in Papua New Guinea in 2002 and trained native people in the jungle. What an experience! In 2003, my relations were not successful. I have since travelled to Europe and Asia for holidays. I love history, culture and spicy foods. I am grateful for an excellent life of interesting experiences and great memories, good and bad.

I now live in Brisbane Australia with my son Christian (19). My eldest daughter Hayley (25) lives in Melbourne and is a professional dancer. My middle daughter Natalie (22) lives alone and studies in University.

I have visited Russia and Ukraine. I took my son to give him bigger experience of life. I hope you enjoy our photo taken at the Mariinsky ballet in Saint Petersburg. I have also been to India, and Canada for skiing with my son. There are so many places yet to see – there is all of South America!

Natalia, until recently I had a very good, enjoyable and secure job. I decided to stop briefly and re-organise my life instead of sitting all day at a computer screen. During this pause in work, I hope to find the love of my life. Together we can decide what, where and the things to do as a joint decision.

I trust that my life story helps you determine my character and "type" of man. I have energy for life. I want an enthusiastic partner to share this passion, but I am not a restless soul. I think that life is too short to waste watching TV or sitting idly, though I sometimes do both these things. I am sure that you understand me.

I am serious in my intentions to find a good woman for marriage. I do not want

to correspond for months. I do not want a virtual Internet romance. I am not looking for a servant or a cook. I want a sincere and loving relationship with a woman with an open, tender passionate heart who can give me all her devotion, her commitment, and her joy. I want to have a family where two can be as one and I can shower her in love.

I know – strong words - but I think I know what is important in life. Such high hopes also means that perhaps the special woman for me doesn't live in my neighbourhood, so I look further into the world.

I have tried to tell about myself. I was honest and direct. Please do not think I am bragging. I want you to know as much about me as possible so you can make your choice with your eyes open.

Everything is OK with me, physically healthy, mentally and sexually; no bad habits and certainly, I do not have problems dating women. I am not rich, but I can certainly work well enough for two to travel together. I will not list the places I wish to travel. I am sure that you have a good imagination.

I admire an intelligent easy-going woman and I do not like vanity. The special lady for me will be adaptable and able to dress like a queen, dine in the best restaurant in Paris, and also be the tourist in a dusty dry village in some strange country. You look like a princess already - do you enjoy camping or 4 star hotels?

I see future life as a combination of travel and experiencing as much as possible and all shared with someone close. I am an optimist. I am well balanced also - sometimes life must not be so serious. I think you understand what I mean. The journey of my life should give you a clear picture of the choices I made and the way I have chosen to live my life and the moral standards I chose. Thanks for reading to the end of this long letter.

Finally, when we die our tombstones will say "Born 1954 - Died 20XX". What is most important is what we did during the "-"! What is your ideas about this?

Kind regards,

James.

Did you actually get through all of that? I am pretty sure it took about three cups of coffee for poor Tatyana to make it to the end of the letter.

Lack of focus on women

Some letters I've seen read like a term paper, as if you were forced to write it – you scrambled up something just to get a passing grade, and you weren't even paying attention when the teacher was giving out the assignment. Such letters will never help you establish a personal connection, even if you write to the most desperate woman.

A very common occurrence is when a man creates a template (which generally includes all possible mistakes), and when he sends it out, he forgets to replace the original name in the letter with the name of the next woman to whom he is writing. Put yourself in a woman's place for just a minute – would you like being called by another guy's name? What would it make you feel and think about the person writing the letter? Such instances send women the message that you are not that interested, not very reliable, and definitely not worth getting to know.

While it may come as a surprise to some, all people like attention – they like being appreciated, they like being acknowledged, they like being noticed. This is the basic principle of any communication with women – make them feel special, appreciated, admired. If you are writing to a woman, make sure that you make your letters about her – her profile, interests, and events in her life. That is how you start a dialogue, a dialogue is what leads to relationships, and relationships grow into commitment and a happy future (after a few pages we will discuss in detail how to do it quickly and easily).

To grab a woman's attention, your letter must be different – this means no cheesy clichés, this means letting your personality sparkle, this means making the lady reading your letter feel special. An impossible task, you think? Not at all. You can easily accomplish this by saying the right thing, by giving the right kind of information, and by knowing how to respond to your woman's profile and letters – we will talk about this in detail in just a minute.

Here is an example of a short, but utterly horrible letter as well:

Hi misskazakistan----

U are a sweetie...are you? :) haha---Its my birthday today when do i get my present :) I don't remember you writing me before, why haven't u? I really haven't had a relationship on here since May 2011 when i was most interested in one girl.

You have a nice butt and beautiful hands. I want your hands in my mouth hahahahaha. Actually my teeth are killing me this week..long story but my dentist is out of town this week. Tomorrow i have an apt. Can you be there to assist? :) Then come home with me :) hmmm

So you are in USA but on a Russian dating site? What's up with that? In USA for 11 years and aren't married? But you must have lived with a guy or something like that...right? Anyway nice to meet you...can i see you on webcam. I dont know how this works with oksana...im sure you have many suitors..be blessed and have a great Sunday sabbath and don't forget to praise the lord...richee rich

I don't think there exists a letter worse than this – it is a compendium of mistakes. The guy is full of himself, he does not show any interest in the woman, he is demanding, pushy, and self-centered. Once again, imagine that such a masterpiece lands in your inbox. If it does not make you want to rip your hair out, you have the nerves of steel (*hint: most women don't!*).

There are several taboo topics you should never – and I mean NEVER – bring up in your communication with the ladies. The most common of them are money, sex, politics, and questioning woman's intentions, for obvious reasons.

I have seen many horrible, bad, so-so, good, and excellent letters and want to share them with you along with an explanation of why they did or didn't work. Templates of such letters will help you avoid the same mistakes and find the perfect formula to get any woman's attention. I am not including these templates in this book for a number of reasons. First, this book is not about writing emails, but about helping you find your perfect Russian bride in 90 days. Also, the skill of writing great emails that get women's attention requires more than a few pages – I have an entire program, a system called "Magnetic Email" that discusses the intricacies of the issue. You can access a free webinar after registering your free profile at *www.OksanaLove.com/Gift.* I want you to be prepared when you begin writing to the woman of your dreams as it is an essential part of future success of your relationship.

Once you receive the templates, you will notice that each one of them is different in nature – this is because women from different categories have different priorities in their lives, they react to different things, they see life differently. Before you approach a woman, you need to understand what drives her, what matters to her. In this case you will be able to give a woman the sense that you "get her", that you understand her and can relate – only then she will feel like she has met a like-minded person. This is very important!

Here are some basic categories of women you will encounter during your search:

- Business woman
- Student
- Single mother
- Divorced woman
- Young professional (age 20-35)
- Woman 35-45
- Woman over 45

Keep in mind that a woman you will write to might fit into several different categories – for example, she may be a businesswoman raising a child on her own. In this case, you would need to mix and match to select the triggers to attract attention of this particular woman; you can browse through several applicable templates and create a perfect message for the particular woman you like.

By the way, when I speak of using triggers, I am not suggesting that you manipulate women – I want you to keep an open mind and to really try to relate to them. You can be successful at conquering women's hearts only when you learn to understand them. When you will be able to feel their struggles, problems, and experiences as if they are your own, you will not even have to put any effort into establishing an emotional connection with these women. And once you've established an emotional connection, any woman will naturally want to be close to you; and women who will feel physical chemistry* will want to be with you forever. Brian Tracy's quote comes to mind: "Successful people are always looking for opportunities to help others. Unsuccessful people are always asking, "What's in it for me?"

Many men often lack confidence when writing to Russian women because these women are... too beautiful. They think that to approach such beautiful women requires a lot of money, buying expensive gifts, and looking like a Hollywood star. It is not true. Of course, women enjoy gifts, they like generous men, but they are more interested in a stable, genuine relationship and finding a man they can rely on. If you try to build a relationship with women based only on gifts, women will feel like you are trying to buy their affection and will keep their distance or they will use you because you permit it, so don't complain that you ran into a gold-digger. Remember that the best way to impress a woman is to be affectionate, attentive, and honest. The devil really is in the details, so small things can make or break your relationship – if you make a woman feel like she is the most important thing to you in the whole world, she will adore you and consider you the best man in the world.

---

*You don't have to look like a movie star. Physical chemistry is about the connection, about the exchange of compatible energy through your touch, kiss or physical contact. I will talk about this in detail in further chapters.

What your Russian bride is not saying

We live in a high-tech world, today most people prefer to begin communication through their computer screen before meeting in person or sharing any personal interaction, even while living in the same city. Needless to say, it is one of the most preferred ways of communication with someone who lives across the ocean. Videos are a great way to gain an insight to what your Russian lady is really like and whether she is right for you. It is quite all right to meet a person virtually first before interacting face-to-face – in fact, there are several advantages to such an approach. You will find them below along with tips on how to make the most of such communication.

Appearance

While some people might consider it superficial, physical attraction is, no doubt, important if you plan to marry someone or form a long-term relationship with. Seeing your lady on video is a great way to see if she is as attractive in life as in her pictures and whether she suits your taste.

Spoken language

Listening is just as important in your video communication as looking. Asking the right questions and listening carefully to what your Russian lady is saying can explain many things to you and help you decide whether the two of you are compatible (*note*: use the tactics from the previous chapter to make sure you relate to a woman you are talking to). Talking live on video is a great way for you to find out all those things that can be sometimes difficult to express in emails: what her dreams are, what her family is like, what kind of life she is looking for, etc. Answers to these questions can really give you a valuable insight into her inner world and whether she is someone you can see yourself living with for the rest of your life.

It is also a great way to talk about some 'sensitive' matters – for example, your relationship, planning a visit, etc. Hearing her voice and seeing the expression on her face when talking about serious matters can give you a clue as to what she really thinks: if she speaks with confidence, it is a great sign; if she avoids the subject or sounds unsure, you will need to pay close attention to what is happening in your relationship.

Personality

One of the greatest benefits videos offer is being able to see someone's true personality. Is your Russian lady serious? Is she cheerful and outgoing? Is she focused on business? For example, if you are looking for an educated, intellectual woman, and your woman only talks of soaps she watches, she is probably not the partner you are looking for. Videos allow you to make such judgments, so both of you can save time if you are not right for each other.

Body language

What is even more important to notice is your Russian lady's body language or mannerisms. Does she have a confident posture? Does she keep her face down because she is shy? Does she fidget nervously? Is she expressive? Does she have a sad look in her eyes? All these things can reveal to you the information about a woman's inner state: whether she is relaxed, depressed, easy-going, etc.

Examining your bride's body language is very important as it can give you information you can't get from letters or photos. It is also a well-known fact that Russians are masters of emotional camouflage – there will be a lot of hide-and-seek in relationships and dating Russian women. However, this doesn't mean such women play games. Historically speaking, Russian "hiding" phenomenon dates back to the regime of Stalin, in 1930's. People were closely monitored by the government and could often be taken away by the government officials for no obvious reasons, especially if they dared to speak their mind against the regime. Many times people simply disappeared with relatives having no idea where their loved ones were taken, and even your closest neighbor could spy and inform against you. This taught people to be very select in what they say and to contain their emotional displays.

These traits were passed from one generation to another behind the "iron curtain" and can still be found today in younger generations. I remember my grandmother saying to my mother – and later me – "Never show your entire ass to your husband", meaning that a woman should not reveal all her emotional secrets to her husband. Another famous Russian saying illustrates this point very well: "A woman has to remain an unread book to her man, so he wants to continue reading it without losing interest."

Thanks to the western influence, women in Eastern Europe began opening up and ridding themselves of the old ideas, yet, in my opinion, it will take several more generations to eliminate the habit of hiding emotions before people can feel free to open up about their thoughts, ideas, and emotions.

You will notice that Russian women who lived in the USA for more than 5 years are quite different from women who still reside in the former Soviet Union. Russian women living in the USA are a lot more open and feel a lot more comfortable talking about their feelings. Women from abroad require some time to get used to such freedom before they can be comfortable and trusting in opening their mind and heart to you.

In light of this, remember a few important things if you feel that your Russian beauty is not opening up to you during your video conversations:

- don't jump to conclusions and don't assume it's your fault!
- it is not that she doesn't trust you, it is about her genetic habit and former lifestyle;
- she will not open up on the first date (actual or virtual);
- she will need time to adjust;
- you need to be patient to gain trust of ANY Russian woman;

------------------------- Resource! -------------------------------

I have recorded for you free video tutorials "The Path to the Russian Heart" which include a guide on reading Russian women's body language (the first lesson in the series talks about this). After watching the video, you will know how to read your Russian woman's postures and what signals about her opening up to you, as well as learn how to keep her relaxed and at ease during your conversation. The series are available to all members of my agency. You will receive the email with details of the video course after you've registered your profile on
www.OksanaLove.com/GIFT

Phone rules

Many men become very nervous at the thought of speaking to their Russian woman on the phone. Indeed, it can be a challenge, but here are a few tips that will help you make this experience pleasant and beneficial.

First, I strongly recommend exchanging several emails before calling your woman, regardless of her location. Emails will help you establish some form of foundation, build excitement and anticipation. Emails are a MUST prior to making a phone call, especially if you are shy, – I would say 5-10 emails is a good number. While you might feel more comfortable communicating through emails, don't drag it out – women like men of action, and if you keep writing instead of taking the next step, a woman might lose interest (this is especially true for USA based women) and wonder if you are real or whether you are really interested in her.

Of course, you might want to call the person straight away, but I don't recommend it. First, you don't know how many people a woman is communicating with. If she suddenly receives a phone call from a man she doesn't really know anything about, awkward moments are guaranteed – not something you want to start your relationship with. Second, without having at least some prior communication which can reveal common interests and give you an idea of your woman's character, a phone conversation might get dull very quickly – it is highly likely that you will not have much to talk about or, worse, will start saying something silly in an attempt to fill up awkward silence.

And, as always, it is my pleasure to give you a perfect recipe to make your phone conversations smooth and easy.

EXCITEMENT is the key to your communication. It is contagious. Remember the times when you were around people who share their excitement with others – didn't you love hearing passionate stories about people's work, their lives, families, and activities? If you are an enthusiastic communicator, women will enjoy being around you – everyone likes to be around people who inspire others.

PREPARATION will make the whole thing easier. Prepare questions and possible conversations topics prior to calling her – then write them down. I've seen it happen too many times: men think they are ready, they have a few ideas of things they want to discuss with their Russian woman, but when they get her on the phone, all their ideas seem to vanish. You might never use your crib sheet, but it is best to have it in case you suddenly blank out. Remember, the girl you will be talking to will be twice as nervous as you, so you might have to take lead in the conversation.

CREATIVITY matters. Everyone asks the same questions in the beginning – where do you work, what about your family, what are you looking for in a partner, etc. No doubt, these are important things, but you can always get to them later. Instead, ask your Russian woman things out of the ordinary – about her dream destination for travel, her goals in life or something else that would be unusual, yet important. Share with her something interesting to attract her attention. Being creative in your discussion is the key to helping her remember you.

SHARING is important. Sometimes our past sorrows and disappointments cause us to close up –we become reluctant to share information about ourselves with others, yet expect them to be open with us. But with such an attitude it is really impossible to create a good relationship – if you don't open up, how will the other person ever get to know you? Also, remember that women (especially Russian women) have a good intuition – if you are not being totally genuine and open, they might feel like you are hiding something and not disclose much about themselves as well. However, remember that there can be too much information. For one, avoid sensitive topics, especially in the beginning of your communication (politics, sex, former partners, money). For another, it is best not to reveal everything about yourself at once. Doing so can be overwhelming – after all, the fun of the dating process is in getting to know each other. Sharing information in stages will allow your Russian woman to get to know you more deeply and focus on the necessary aspects of your personality you may wish to highlight. This will also appeal to your lady's sense of curiosity – she will be intrigued to get to know you further.

LISTENING will get you further than talking. Use the 20 – 80% rule in your conversations – meaning, 20% of talking vs. 80% of listening. If you really want to get to know someone – let them talk. You will be amazed at what you will find out, plus, usually the person doing most of the talking is more likely to feel that there is chemistry in the conversation.

ATTENTION accompanies good listening. When talking to a woman over the phone, refer to things she has mentioned in her profile or emails – this will show her that you actually read what she has to say and you are paying attention.

RELAXATION is important. If you are tense, it will reflect on your communication skills. I have watched many people during their first meetings, whether online or offline, – most of the time both parties are so nervous that the experience becomes unpleasant for both. When you are tense, you are unable to be at your best; you can also create a sense of mistrust in your partner and you will not have a chance to truly get to know each other and have a second meeting. Being relaxed will help you remain confident and put your best foot forward – that's the only way you can truly show strong points of your personality. There are many relaxation techniques: someone chooses yoga, someone uses meditation, yet someone else chooses to have a drink before the meeting. Whatever your strategy, make sure it works and keeps you adequate for genuine communication. You can always take up communication courses as with practice confidence and relaxation will follow.

AVOID PRECONCEPTIONS in your discussions. Getting to know someone from a different country is a certain way to expand your horizons, however, stereotypes often get in the way of really getting to know the other person. While you might be used to doing things a certain way or following certain traditions, other cultures can offer you a different perspective – and at times teach you something important. If you get busy comparing how differently you do certain things, you will miss out on the beauty of communication.

NEGATIVITY is out of the question. Don't fill your conversation with complaints, criticism or other expressions of negativity. The initial moments of communication and meeting are important; use them to the fullest to make a good impression. While we all have our moments of weakness, it is best to first establish connection with your Russian lady before you pour out the sorrows of your heart.

FINISH WITH A SMILE. It is important to say good-bye at the point when you both are in a good mood and enjoying the conversation. The way you finish your conversation is the way your women will remember you. Finishing on a positive note (ideally with a joke) will keep the woman smiling for the next several hours, and every time she will think about you, she will definitely do it with a smile.

LIMIT your first conversation to 20 minutes at maximum – this will keep your woman from becoming overwhelmed and send her a message that you have a bunch of important things to do (Russian women love men who have busy lives full of important things to do!).

SET THE TIME for the next phone call, specify date and time ahead. Many people forget to do this. Conversations remain as if unfinished and neither man nor woman knows whether or not there was a connection or what to expect next. You can say something like: "This was fun, thanks so much for finding time to talk to me. What do you think if I call you next Thursday? Would that day work for you? And if so, would 5 pm work for you or would 8 pm be better?"

The language challenge

Language barrier is one of the main obstacles in your search for a foreign wife, however, it is a problem only if you make it a problem – I say this after having observed hundreds of couples, some of which were able to communicate and get along even when a woman didn't know hardly a word of English.

In fact, I've noticed that those couples where a woman barely speaks English are more stable; such relationships are often fueled by humorous situations partners face with regard to the "issue". Such couples are generally closer physically, and their intimacy level is much higher than with the ones who speak the same language. It might seem absurd, but there is a simple explanation to this phenomena: couples with language "issues" have to look for other forms of communication during which they touch each other more (pointing at things, looking into a dictionary together and touching cheeks) – physical contact becomes the norm, while couples where both partners speak the language often fall behind trying to discuss what is acceptable.

I introduced the couple in the photo during one of my tours in the Dominican Republic. Marina did not speak a word of English, literally zero. She and her now husband connected at once, they were always smiling, holding hands, looking for words in a dictionary, trying to build phrases, and communicating just fine, even making jokes. I offered them the help of an interpreter, but they refused. When I asked Marina how they were able to communicate, she said "We just try to find words in a dictionary and use gestures, and when we face awkward silence, we just cover it with kisses". Well, you can see from the photos that they had many awkward silent

moments, but something tells me her man (now husband) didn't mind a bit.

I am not saying that you shouldn't talk – it is important to discuss certain issues to understand whether you are right for each other. However, to determine chemistry and attraction, you need more than words – to be more precise, you need to kiss, dance, touch, and smell.

We all have intuition, but sometimes we choose to disregard it by listening to our logic and mind instead. Scientists have already proven that when two people kiss, the mix of their saliva creates a certain chemical reaction. This reaction has a specific taste and smell, but it also stimulates certain emotional reactions which can be positive or negative. So, when we are with the wrong person, a kiss with that person will feel wrong, it will taste bad, it will not be enjoyable, simply because genetically we are with someone whose genes aren't a good match for us – it is nature telling us: "Stop! Reproduction in this combination will not be right." But when we are with the right person (genetically speaking), our entire body responds to that kiss, we don't want to stop, we shiver, we want to get closer and closer. In this case, your children will be smart and beautiful (should you go further than a kiss, of course). I am certain, you know what I am talking about, and you can surely remember all the lovely kisses you've shared as well as kisses that felt very, very wrong.

The same is true for two people touching each other. Skin is our biggest organ, it is very sensitive to outside factors. If we communicate on the same wavelength, levels of our body energy complement each other. Have you ever wanted to run away for no obvious reasons from someone the minute you met them? This was your skin accepting signals from another person's body and telling you that you are not compatible. If you want to test your compatibility with a woman, touching is a great way to do so; if you are looking for an opportunity to touch her, then asking her to dance is the perfect way to see how comfortable you are with your potential partner.

Smell is another factor that affects our chemistry with another person. I am referring to an individual body aroma. You certainly have been in a situation where you didn't want to be close to someone because their smell wasn't appealing – again, this is your body telling you that you are not compatible with this person, sexually or otherwise. Unfortunately, many men try to force relationships with gorgeous women even if they don't feel any chemistry; needless to say, such relationships almost never work out.

Let's get back to the language issue, nonetheless. If you are still concerned about being able to communicate, here is something that should put you at ease. A foreign language is mandatory in most schools, colleges, and universities in Russia and Ukraine. English is one of the most common languages taught, followed by German and French. Specialized schools teach foreign languages from grade one, other schools introduce languages from about fourth or fifth year.

This means that even if your woman did not attend a specialized language school, she would have had at least a few years of exposure to a foreign language. However, if she did not have a chance to practice it or graduated a while ago, she could simply forget what she knew or lack confidence in using the language. This is where she will need your help, to remind her of what she knows and help her practice the language. But first, you must build her confidence and encourage practicing the language in a comfortable environment. This means, you must let her know that it is okay to make mistakes and give her your full support.

Basically, about 15% of women will be able to speak English well, about 20% will have at least basic vocabulary, and the rest will at least be able to understand some of what is being said to them, given that you speak slowly and clearly. You are likely to find more English speaking women in larger cities than in rural areas. In many situations, even if a woman is convincing you she does not know the language, it can simply be her lack of confidence and fear of sounding funny.

Once you know how much English your lady can speak, you can help her in more tangible ways when it comes to improving her language skills. If she knows the language well, but simply lacks practice, you can correct this by frequent communication and some basic self-help books and materials. If her knowledge is less or very limited, you might think about hiring a tutor along with buying some language-learning software for her.

Now is a good time to share with you information about a special language program developed by my good friend specifically for "Russian brides". Julia is a former "Russian bride" herself who married an American gentleman and now lives in New York. She knows what Russian women face when they come to America. Formerly an English teacher, she agreed to help me design a language program which would be aimed at Russian women with limited language knowledge who want to marry a foreigner. This program can help any woman, with any level language knowledge to speak at least basic English within 2-3 months - I've seen it happen to just about every girl who has taken this course.

------------------------------- Resource! -------------------------------
You can check out her "English for "Brides" program at *www.UsaLanguageAcademy.com*

She currently works on "Russian for Grooms" designed specifically for men looking to find and marry a Russian woman.

This isn't plain advertising. I recommend this course for a number of reasons. First, it works. Second, your woman might be unable to afford English lessons even if she wants to learn the language. Most English tutors/classes charge from $15 per hour of studies; to learn the language, one should take 2-3 lessons a week; that's at least $120 a month with an average salary being $150-200 a month. Once you meet a woman you are seriously interested in, even if you don't get this particular course, you should consider helping her with learning the language by paying for English classes.

Whatever the situation with her language skills, it is important for you to realize that you have to be patient and understanding while she learns the language. Do not show your frustration if the process seems to move too slowly for you, it will only discourage your sweetheart. Make sure that you are supportive of all her efforts. You might also consider learning some basic Russian to make your Russian bride feel more at ease. You don't have to become fluent, but learning a few basic phrases and words will help both of you feel more comfortable while communicating. Julia is now developing a program for gentlemen who want to marry a Russian girl; in it, she will help English-speaking "grooms" to learn Russian language. This is a great chance for you surprise your sweetheart and her parents by your knowledge of her language, to show her that you are serious about her, and increase her confidence in learning a foreign language as well – when she hears your accent in Russian, she will not feel so bad about her stumbling English.

Please, remember, language should not be the deciding factor in your relationship. Yes, it is important for communication, but it is something that can be learned. It is much more important for you to find a person with the qualities you are looking for, as personal traits are a lot harder to cultivate than learning a foreign language.

Let me finish by sharing some humour from my personal archive. This happened during my second week of living in America. I was staying with my fiancé, he left for work leaving me at home on my own. I browsed through all cabinets in search of toothpaste (I didn't know enough language to read the labels, so I had to rely on my sense of taste and smell). I brushed my teeth with something that was very minty, soft and warm, very surprised that American toothpaste is that much stronger than anything I've tried in Russia. However, I didn't question it – I've heard Americans use kick-ass products. My mouth remained very minty for quite a while, and when my fiancé returned home, I expressed my surprise as to the strength of toothpaste he uses. He asked me to show him the tube, and when he saw it, his eyes got huge, he started asking me if I was feeling ok, checking my temperature and pupils. It turned out I had brushed my teeth with… BenGay! Luckily, I wasn't hurt in any way. But after this occurrence, my fiancé separated all the tubes in the cabinet and instructed me not to touch anything on the right side to be safe.

But that's not the end of the story… My mother, who doesn't speak much English, visited me in the USA a few years later. We stayed with some friends over a weekend (the wife was a Russian who had married an American). One morning my mother walked out of her bathroom saying "Americans sure use strong toothpaste!" – I don't need to explain what happened, do I?

And another short story about challenges of pronunciation. When someone is learning a foreign language, it is easy to confuse some words, especially if they are very close in spelling. Remember my excitement about McDonald's? One day I was busy telling my fiancé and his friends how much I enjoyed McDonald's buggers (yes, you read it right!). I get very passionate when I talk about something exciting, so it took me a few minutes to notice smiles and friendly laughter as I spoke of buggers instead of burgers.

CHAPTER 7: HOW TO…

Feeling shy? Start dating hot girls

Having coached hundreds of people, I see the same pattern over and over again – the biggest issue most men have in approaching women is… shyness. Many of us, including me, deal with the same issue. As a professional matchmaker and an expert in introducing, inspiring, and coaching people, I feel rather comfortable speaking in front of groups of people about my work – I feel comfortable even speaking on camera. But when it comes to my personal life and personal affairs, oh boy, I get so shy, you wouldn't believe.

I've noticed that the same thing is true for many professionals, regardless of their line of work. Men might speak in front of hundreds of people every day, they might be the center of attention in their circle of friends, but when it comes to starting a conversation with a gorgeous woman about personal things, something happens and they suddenly become shy and not so talkative. It is understandable – you blush, your heart is racing, you are dealing with emotions.

The reason for this is hidden in our subconscious stereotypes about relationships. We've all faced rejection, we've all mended broken hearts, so, when it is time to meet a gorgeous woman, it is natural that your subconscious starts telling you that you will be rejected again or that the relationship will never work. But if you really want to marry a beautiful Russian woman, you must stop such thoughts.

Think back to when you were a child – did you ever think that things were too good, too expensive or too much for you? Certainly, not! You must assume the same attitude again. Stop predicting what might happen, especially if you expect the outcome to be negative.

You must also learn to deal with rejection. People who have overcome shyness constantly step outside their comfort zone and never take rejection personally. Instead, they quickly draw conclusions and try again. Such people shake off negative aspects of any experience, learn from it, and ignore what others think.

Remember, the more time you devote to something, the more comfortable you will feel doing it. I am willing to bet that you feel much more confident at your job/business desk than speaking with a gorgeous woman – this is because you are a professional and work in the same field day in and day out, but you haven't had an opportunity to gain the same experience when it comes to dating (you tried, you faced rejection you feel like you failed, and, therefore, quit until you were able to work up enough courage to try it again).

This is where online dating has a significant advantage over traditional dating – it makes contact and communication so much easier, because you don't have to face rejection face-to-face. You can send emails to several women, and even if half of them doesn't reply – who cares? You still have so many more to talk to. Of course, emails don't solve the issue of being shy and feeling awkward when meeting in person or speaking on the phone with your Russian woman. But what they do is establish a foundation for your relationship and future communication – you will most certainly be more comfortable speaking to a woman with whom you've exchanged letters for several months as opposed to making a date with a complete stranger.

Writing to several women is also a great confidence booster – you will not only feel more comfortable writing to gorgeous Russian women, but you will also discover that they are much more receptive to your messages than you expected and want to get to know you. Have you experienced speed dating? In the beginning it seems like communication is a struggle, but once you've spoken to a few people, you feel so much more confident and it becomes a lot easier to talk to other women, regardless of their looks. The same happens with online dating – once you've emailed several women, you gain confidence and start having fun. It also helps to understand that there are many women looking for the same thing you are, so if something doesn't work out with one person, there will be many others interested in talking to you.

I prefer to build a relationship with someone via emails before meeting in person. I'd like to share with you a tip that helped me many times when I wasn't feeling too confident about getting to know someone: make a list of questions you would like to ask the person you are trying to get to know, keep that list nearby and feel free to expand it at any moment. It seems that finding things to stimulate discussion (questions, in particular) is the biggest challenge in email correspondence – having this list handy will save you from such troubles. Use the two lists you have created since you began reading this book (qualities you'd like to see in your perfect woman and qualities you possess which might make you attractive to women) as a starting point – discuss items in those lists to find out whether a particular woman is right for you and to promote yourself.

You must remember that Russian women are straight forward; many of them don't like to play games. Don't be afraid to ask questions. By asking questions you will learn more about the woman to whom you are writing as well as show your interest in her – every woman, a gorgeous or an average-looking one, likes attention. By asking a few questions, you'll create an opportunity for a dialogue, allowing your woman to share her world with you.

Most women will be happy to answer your questions even on touchy subjects, provided your questions are respectful and tactful. As you know, Russian women don't like men using drugs. If I were addressing the issue, this is what I would say: "There is something I would like to ask you. I don't mean to be disrespectful, but I am looking for a serious relationship and think it is important to be honest from the start. Can you, please, tell me what you think about people who use drugs? I appreciate your answer and understanding, thank you for your honesty." This is just an example, of course, but it does the job – you tactfully address an important issue without beating around the bush. Of course, you can also add an explanation as to why you asked the question – you can be sure, it will be accepted with understanding.

A gift from a perfect gentleman

Several years ago I made a date with someone I met on a dating website. I have been working crazy hours for several months and was pretty much sleeping in my office. I was tired and exhausted and felt that I really just needed to get out. This gentleman and I exchanged a few emails and set a date that same day. I was looking for someone to chat to and have a few drinks with, just to have a break from work. This man was nothing like my dream man: bald, not attractive at all, simple, an ordinary guy with an ordinary boring job as a bookkeeper – I thought he would do as someone to have a conversation with. When I saw him, I knew there wouldn't be a second date…

Three weeks later I believed that I was deeply in love, and 8 months later I was engaged to the guy. He was masterful at always surprising me with gifts. He couldn't afford anything expensive on a bookkeeper's salary, but he created an important and meaningful moment every time he did something for me. Yet, everything he did was very simple and easy, so there is no reason you can't follow suit.

The most important thing about him was that he could listen and was observant. He listened to every word I shared with him, right from the first date. I mentioned that I was tired and burned out on work and needed to get my mind off it because I had difficulty sleeping as my mind continued to focus on work on auto pilot and I often felt like I simply got stuck in a rut, unable to find solutions. On our second date (the very next day!) he gave me a book "If Buddha Got Stuck: A Handbook for Change on a Spiritual Path". This showed me that he really listened to what I said. It was a small present, but since I am a ferocious reader (something I shared with him the night before), he thought it would be perfect for me. The book is still on my night stand, and I read it every time when I need to switch my mind off work – it works like a charm.

At the time I was working on a serious project, but it seemed that everything I did was wrong. I started to lose confidence in myself and, although I never mentioned it to him, he seemed to understand what was going on – the next book that ended up in my hands was called "Profiles of Female Geniuses" and spoke about 13 creative women who changed the world. But the real surprise was on the inside cover of the book – a note that said "To my genius who changed my world. I believe in you!" That note was a breath of fresh air I needed so badly! Needless to say, the book served its purpose – after I finished it, I knew that I was ready to do some amazing things as well. Oksanalove vacations for singles in the Caribbean appeared a few months later, leading to 43 engagements within a year. Sadly, this project was the reason for our breakup because I made a horrible mistake when I chose my clients over this man and decided to spend over a year overseas, but that is a story for my memoirs.

To get back on track, books weren't the only thing he gave me. He also gave me a CD labeled "Just for you - just listen" – he made a compilation of romantic songs that made me feel warm and cozy inside every time I listed to the music (maybe, at that point I started feeling close to this man).

He loved to take photos of me, of us together. I didn't mind and didn't suspect what was coming – a week or so later I received several cute packages of M&M's with our photos and amazing phrases of admiration and love on the cover.

Every time we met, there were flowers, soft music, and candle-light dinner. This man knew that I needed to recoup, to recharge my batteries, and he made everything in his power to create that atmosphere for me. How did he know? He listened. He paid attention to my every word, to every memory I shared, to every thought I voiced.

He never allowed me to pay on our dates and made sure to take me to places I mentioned I hadn't visited before, but wanted to visit. I once mentioned that I like exotic foods and have never tried crocodile or snake meat – at the very first opportunity my date took me to a Creole festival where I could satisfy my curiosity. I have told him that as a former pro dancer I loved to dance but didn't enjoy clubs that much – he took me to dance classes, to a salsa festival, and to live concerts hosted in the parks of the city.

He once took me out without saying where we are going, although asked me to wear something comfortable. When we reached our destination, he surprised me with a picnic (a basket full of salads, wine, cheeses, plates, and silverware – of course, there was also a rose in a glass – on a cozy blanket in a serene setting). He was the only man who has ever done something like this for me, and it was the most fantastic romantic moment. With every move he tried to make my life easy and relaxing, which I appreciated greatly since I was so busy at work.

Why am I telling you this? First, to show you that special gifts or moments don't require a huge budget. Second, to say to you, as a woman, that such small gestures are often more meaningful than one grand event a year. Finally, such approach is something you definitely want to implement when dating Russian women – it will make you stand out from the crowd and make a lasting impression, guaranteed.

Some of you might say: "Yes, I know, but I am not creative or imaginative and could never come up with something like that." Well, that's just an excuse. You don't have to invent the wheel, your lady will give you all the answers – you just have to listen! Remember different categories of women we spoke about? Use that information to relate to her challenges, her needs, and her emotions, and every gift you give will be perfect.

This will get you a young Russian bride

Have you ever wondered why many Russian women would consider an older gentleman for a husband? I give you seven main reasons (some are obvious, while others are simply shocking) as to why this happens.

Reason #7 – Maturity is not an option, but a rule.

Russian women have to mature fast. I've already explained to you why: they take care of the house, work full time, provide assistance to their parents (especially if they are older), put a lot of effort into looking beautiful, and have little help from men who expect that all their needs will be taken care of regardless of how tired a woman is at the end of the day.

Naturally, a little girl watching her mother working full-time, completing all house work without fancy equipment (dishes are still hand-washed, even some linen washing is done the old-fashioned way), and finding time to give attention to all members of the family, matures a lot faster from the involvement in all these activities. Young girls learn even more responsibility if they have siblings as they often help their mother take care of their younger brothers or sisters.

As a result, when young women begin to look for a partner, they are not very interested in men their age who are still basically big children. Instead, they want a man who has learned responsibility and can appreciate his woman's care instead of taking it for granted.

Reason # 6 – Gaining self-confidence.

A large part of this has to do with sexual interest which men and women perceive differently, especially with age. For women sex is not as big of an issue since they have to deal with times when it is out of the question during pregnancy and childbirth. For men sex drive is an integral part of life. Older men often become concerned about the decrease of their sexual drive. Having a young girlfriend or wife often helps them boost their self-esteem, feel young again and become more energetic because women of their own age cannot do the same.

Young women often choose relationships with older men because they lack confidence – they often feel they are not good enough for younger men as such men often put women down and are unfaithful. But once in a relationship with an older man, a young woman also gets a boost of confidence. Instead of being with someone who uses and takes advantage of her, she finds a mature man who can appreciate her, who cares for her and protects her.

If you find yourself in a relationship with a much younger woman, remember that you will benefit from such relationship only if you give your partner maximum support and encouragement. Your confidence has direct influence over her self-confidence and vice versa.

Reason # 5 – Romance.

Young men with raging hormones mainly focus on sex forgetting about romance which women of all ages welcome and adore. Older men, having vast experience, appreciate emotional connection more than plain sex. Grooming, gifts, flowers – with age romance becomes necessary, giving a man an opportunity to woo and feel like a courteous caballero.

Women – especially after 35-40 years of age, once their children are grown up, – see their partner as someone to whom they can pass on their care, even maternal feelings. A woman's care of her spouse now moves to a new level, she is able to give him more love and affection. If her older husband now surrounds her with romance instead of focusing only on sex, she will again feel like a real woman, who is loved and surrounded by affection.

Reason #4 – Men remain younger than women of their age.

It is well-known that girls grow up faster than boys. Think back to school years: when boys were still going through adolescent struggles, girls already became young women who wore make up, showed interest in older boys, and had more mature bodies. Girls also develop social skills faster; they are more likely to compromise.

The same progression remains as women get older – they generally age and become older faster than men. If you look at the couples where partners are of the same age, men generally have more energy and look at least 10 years younger than their wives.

Jeff Wilser in his book "The Maxims of Manhood" suggests using the following formula to calculate a perfect age difference: take a man's age, divide it by two, and add 7. That is supposed to be the best age of a woman for a man when they start a relationship. So, let's say you are 50 years old: $50 : 2 + 7 = 32$. So, a 32 year old woman should be an ideal match for you. The older you are, the more the age gap between you and your perfect partner, provided you have qualities of a "real man" to handle such an age difference (I will discuss this a bit later). A word of caution: this formula should be used only if you plan to have children as it was developed based on women's genetics – a woman has to be young enough to get pregnant and bring a child to this world. So, realistically speaking, women at 40+ have fewer chances to get pregnant to fulfill their genetic purpose in life, while men remain boys and can get a woman pregnant at any age.

Reason # 3 – Sexual aspect.

It is very simple – young men, with a few exceptions, simply don't have as much experience as older men. Older men know not only how to romance a woman, but also how to please her sexually. It is no secret that it takes women longer to become aroused and that they require different stimulation than men. Since older men are not in as much of a hurry as younger men who are guided by raging hormones, they can allow more time for a woman to become aroused before sharing in intimacy. And since a younger woman is a natural stimulant for an older man, he remains just as active as his young competitor.

Reason # 2 – Respect.

Let's look at a couple where a man of 65-70 years married a lady of 35-40. As he becomes older, he becomes less critical, of others and himself, he is wise, and has learned not to sweat the small stuff in life. She dreams of having balance and serenity in life, without petty quibbles, and wants to have confidence in future. The two are a good fit for each other's expectations, and the woman gets something she probably wouldn't from a younger man – respect for her individuality, dreams, and ambitions.

Reason # 1 – I need a father!

This is perhaps the most important psychological factor as to why Russian women feel comfortable in a relationship with an older man. It is said that if a woman marries a much older man, she is subconsciously looking for a father figure.

Based on the statistics of my agency, approximately 70 – 80% of Russian women were raised without a father for one reason or another. In some cases their father left home for another woman, in others he simply was never around or didn't put any effort into raising a daughter because it is a woman's responsibility to raise children. Psychologists often say that our childhood shapes our adulthood, so it is natural that many girls raised without a father look for a father figure in their future partner on a subconscious level. An older man can give her the kind of attention she never had as a child, he can give her protection as a father would, he is also someone to guide and teach a young woman. Such a man can provide comfort; he will cherish her as his little girl and give her love she did not receive when she was younger.

However, it is not enough to just be older to make a great husband for a Russian woman. If you wish to build such a relationship with a younger woman, you must be ready to show maturity, to become her mentor and teacher, to bear responsibility, and, of course, to become a caring father to your children. If you show these qualities, she WILL respect and love you, and she will always be loyal and faithful to you.

A relationship with a young Russian woman is not for everyone. You need to know what to expect. Many men who marry younger women suddenly face unexpected challenges and fears such as:

- She will leave me for a younger man.
- She loves me because of my social status and wealth.
- I feel guilty with regard to my ex-wife and the family I left behind (if you left them for a younger woman).
- I feel guilty about not being with my children.
- I become angry and jealous every time a younger man compliments my young wife.

People around you probably won't make it easy for you either. You can expect the following if you choose to marry a younger woman:

- Everyone around you will be judging. Especially if most of your friends are married to women of their own age.
- All married women – coworkers, friends, family – will be questioning your wife's intentions, fueling her fears, and trying to make her feel inferior.
- Your married friends, if they are true friends, will be happy for you, yet jealous at the same time, as they do not have the luxury of returning to a sexy, beautiful, young woman every day after work.
- Your single friends will be happy for you, but they also might hit on her – many friendships were ruined that way.

- Anywhere you go people will be asking you if she is your daughter.

It doesn't seem like a big deal, but it can really take toll on a relationship. You need to be prepared to deal with all these things, you must be confident, you must learn to turn a deaf ear to your friends and family in some instances. If you care what others think or are not sure you can handle these things, DO NOT BEGIN A RELATIONSHIP WITH A YOUNGER WOMAN. It might sound harsh, but your marriage will not sustain the pressure if you listen to others and question your relationship and your wife's motives.

Now let's do a little test which can help you calculate whether you are prepared to date and marry a younger lady. If the test shows that you are not 100% ready, you will know which aspects your need to work on. This is what you need to do: mark "agree" or "disagree" in response to each of the 30 questions below.

	Agree	Disagree
1. I have high self-esteem.		
2. I respect opinions of others, even if I disagree.		
3. I like to read and patiently teach others how to improve their life.		
4. I am a sexually healthy man.		
5. I respect myself too much to get involved in a relationship with a woman who doesn't have respect for herself.		
6. I don't care what other's think.		
7. I understand that younger women need to be treated differently; they should be pampered with designer clothes,		

shopping, and salon treatments.		
8. I think impeccable clothes are necessary to make a good impression not only on women, but on potential business partners as well.		
9. Young women are naïve and stupid.		
10. Paying for woman's beauty treatments is not an expense, but an investment.		
11. I am in an excellent physical shape and take care of my health.		
12. I bear authority, coworkers ask me for advice.		
13. I am a romantic, I know how to create a romantic atmosphere or know when to hire someone to do it for me and my sweetheart.		
14. I am attentive; I remember or have someone remind me about all holidays and important events for my loved ones.		
15. I am a financially stable man.		
16. I don't have patience for people, if they don't get me right away, they must be dumb.		
17. Everyone has unique talents; they can become prominent with just a little help in developing them.		
18. I don't think I deserve interest from much younger women.		
19. It is important for my friends and family to accept my wife.		

20. I love to give gifts, it sincerely brings me pleasure.		
21. My wardrobe is impeccable, I like looking stylish and modern.		
22. I think younger women should be treated no different that women of my own age.		
23. Young women don't know much, they need to listen and do as I say.		
24. Life is too short to get stressed over things. Fix what you can, don't stress over something you can't change.		
25. I can't tolerate stupid people, I have to explain to them what they don't understand and why they are wrong.		
26. I don't think sex is important for women, it is only important for a man.		
27. People at work respect me and value my opinion.		
28. I am overweight, but it is all in my bad genes, I can't do anything about it. A woman will just have to love me for the way I am.		
29. What I drive matters. I have to have a vehicle that reflects my status and shows that I am in charge.		
30. I love to mentor and would be glad to help to a young lady to become successful at whatever her passions are.		

Some of these questions seem similar and ask about the same things in a variety of ways. Some of them reflect inner values, while others focus on a mental position, others are just fun and give you something to think about. All this is done to give you the most accurate result. Now, let's calculate your score.

Give yourself 3 points for every "agree," except questions 9, 16, 18, 19, 22, 23, 25, 26, 28 – if you marked any of them as "agree", mark "0".
Give yourself 3 points for every "disagree" in response to questions 9, 16, 18, 19, 22, 23, 25, 26, 28.
Add points from both columns and add 10 bonus points to your score to get the total.

If your total is 85 +, you have a good chance to meet, date, and have a relationship with a younger woman.
If your score is lower, go back and reflect on the points for which you received "0" – I suggest that you try to implement positive statements in your life or remove negative aspects if the statement is negative. The questions 9, 16, 18, 19, 22, 23, 25, 26,28 are an indication of aggression, intolerance, disrespect, low self-esteem, being concerned about other people's opinion, and lack of taking responsibility for your own life. These qualities will not help you meet a younger woman or create a relationship with her. Such qualities as respect, tolerance, patience, generosity, high self-esteem, and accountability are a must to establish a successful relationship with a younger woman.

You really should be able to tick off every point on this list before you start building a relationship with a younger woman. Don't think that I am being cruel – my experience shows that otherwise you have little chances of making such relationship work, so I am just trying to save you time, money, and heart ache. If you feel you lack some qualities, you can always develop them with enough patience and motivation.

------------------------------- Resource! -------------------------------
To meet magnificent, beautiful, and ambitious young ladies interested in a serious relationship visit *www.OksanaLove.com/gift*. Register your profile to access instantly photos and videos pre-qualified women.

CHAPTER 8: TURNING DATING INTO MARRIAGE

Is your Russian bride ready to settle with you?

Now that you've found a wonderful Russian woman you want to meet in person, you need to know how to determine whether she is ready to settle down and if she likes you.

The most important thing for you to remember is that your Russian woman will not make the first move. As you remember, Russian women are very traditional, so even if your lady likes you a lot, she will wait for you to initiate a phone conversation, a video chat, and, especially, a personal meeting. Along with that you must also know that a Russian woman will NEVER turn down a personal meeting if she is sincere and truly interested in you. If you are corresponding with a woman on a dating site and have offered to meet in person, but she finds excuse after excuse to postpone the meeting, you can be certain that you are either being scammed or wasting your time.

How soon is an interested woman ready to see you in person? Instantly! It is a natural human reaction to want things right this second. It is like asking someone when they want to become happy – I doubt you'll ever hear: "Three months from now". A woman who is genuinely attracted to you and has nothing to hide will be ready to meet you the minute you propose to meet. Don't confuse this with situations when a woman has to juggle personal circumstances of some sort to ensure she can give you adequate attention. For example, you ask if your woman wants to meet and get in response: "You are welcome to come right now, but I will be able to spend more time with you in a month when I can take time off from work". This is definitely something to be excited about – she wants to make sure she can spend as much time with you as possible which is a clear sign of her interest. Below you will find some information that will help you make informed decisions.

If you want to know whether your woman is ready to meet you, these are the things to watch for:

- She talks of travel and asks if you have plans to travel anywhere in the near future (of course, the smart thing to say is that you would want to visit her country because she is there).
- She asks how far you live from her and how long it would take you to get to her country.
- She asks about your leave and how often you take long trips.
- She asks if you've told your parents or friends about her.
- She says that she told her friends or parents about you, and they think you are handsome, interesting, etc.
- If you haven't written in a few days, she sends you her last email again or inquires whether everything is all right with you.
- Once you mention that you want to come over, she asks about the details of your trip (when you plan to arrive, where you will stay, etc.).
- She refers to your letters things you've discussed previously and remembers every detail because she wants to participate in your life.

A woman is ready to commit to you if she talks about the following things:

- She talks about wanting to create a family.
- She talks about having children and how soon she would want it to happen.
- She asks you if you are interested in having children.
- She is genuinely interested in learning about your life, in particular, about your family. She asks about them during every conversation.
- She asks about life in your country, about your family traditions.

Some other things will give you a clear indication that a woman is ready to settle:

- She has worked at the same place for a while as opposed to changing jobs frequently.

- She has a vision of what she wants her future life/career to be as opposed to trying to figure out what she wants to do with her life.
- She takes responsibility for her actions/life.

Of course, if you still have doubts, it is always a good idea to find a tactful way to discuss her intentions and the future of your relationship. If you choose to approach this topic, be sure that you ask things in a way that will not offend your woman – if she is truly interested and you sound as if you question her, you have all chances to ruin a perfectly fine relationship.

Here, there, anywhere

When my clients find women they are interested in, they frequently have difficulty deciding where to have their first meeting. Many of them want to have a woman visit their country to show her what her possible future might be and to see whether she would be able to adapt to new living conditions. Others find it exciting and exotic to visit a woman's country and really enjoy seeing where she comes from. Many couples consider meeting on a neutral territory to be the best option.

Since it is often difficult if not impossible for women from Russia and Ukraine to travel to the United States due to financial and visa limitations, I will not discuss this option. However, I will outline in detail advantages and disadvantages of visiting your woman's country and meeting on a neutral territory.

MEETING IN HER COUNTRY

ADVANTAGES	DISADVANTAGES
- A woman will feel more comfortable at her home town, especially if she has never traveled overseas. - Meeting her family and friends is a great chance to show them that you are a	- You have no chance to see how she would adapt in a foreign country. - There is no way to escape routine problems as you could if both of you were on vacation (for example, your

good choice for their daughter. It will be easier for your bride and her family to deal with distance if her family feels you will take good care of her.

- It is a good chance for you to find out what your bride will be like in a few years – after all, if you want to know what you wife will look like 20 years from now, take a look at her mother. Jokes aside, by visiting her family you will be able to see what is important in her life, who has the main role, who makes decisions, how her father is being treated – and that's exactly what you can expect.
- You can see if she is what she said she is. Being on her own territory, your woman will act natural, so you will see her true personality.
- Visiting your lady's home country will give you a good understanding of your cultural differences, which can help avoid misunderstandings in future.
- Meeting her friends will tell you more about who she is as a person (in Russia there is a saying "Tell me who your friends are, and I will tell you who you are").
- Seeing her home will tell you how well she takes care of it, what her preferences are in decorating/lifestyle. Pay attention to her book shelves and photographs – they will

woman might have to go to work, keep prior commitments, etc.).
- You need a visa to enter all Former Soviet Union countries, except Ukraine.
- Not knowing the language or traditions of the country you are visiting can cause all sorts of misunderstandings and awkward moments. For example, men often get uncertain because they don't know what woman's friends or family members are really saying.
- Long flights (very long flights!). It can take up to 28 hours to get to Kazakhstan from the US, for example.
- You will spend money. In many cases, pricing might come as a shock to you. For example, I have heard numerous complaints from foreign men about how expensive accommodation is in Ukraine.
- Many of her friends might be forceful in giving advice or sharing their opinion of you, if it is dictated by jealousy, such "advisers" can easily ruin a potential relationship
- If you are not careful, you will be taken advantage of in a financial sense – foreigners are often charged through a "special pricing structure" (normally 10 times higher than regular prices).
- Food might be difficult to adjust to. Many foreigners

tell you more about your sweetheart than a thousand words.

- She might be able to negotiate better deals on accommodation, souvenirs, etc. to save you money during the visit.
- Traveling abroad is a great way to plan a meeting with several ladies if you are not committed to a particular woman. You can meet them without feeling "stuck" with a particular person. Even if you are interested only in one woman, you can meet other women from the city/region if something goes wrong during your meeting.

complain of upset stomach, some even lost weight due to the total cleansing of the system.

- The number of beautiful available women might get you confused and distracted from the one you originally came to visit. It can also be the reason for a break up.
- You will be limited in the opportunities of surprising your woman in a romantic sense (i.e. planning a picnic or a trip, even booking a restaurant).
- Discomfort of being in a new, different environment can distract you from the original goal of your trip and cause you to focus on discomfort instead of building the relationship.

MEETING ON A NEUTRAL TERRITORY
(Better if it is a romantic destination – for example, the Caribbean)

ADVANTAGES	DISADVANTAGES
- Nothing can beat a date in a romantic setting on a tropical island. - This is your chance to do something truly amazing for your woman. Few women get a chance to travel, some of them have never seen an ocean; in most countries sea vacations are considered a vacation of quality and	- The number of women to meet is limited. If something goes wrong during your meeting(s), you might not have a chance to enjoy your vacation. - If something goes wrong between you and your woman, being together in a fairly secluded area can be unpleasant and tense.

elite level.

- Both of you will be relaxed and will not be bothered by routine tasks. When you visit a woman in her home country, she will most likely have commitments to keep (children, work, studies, family), so you will get to spend 2-3 hours a day with her at best. Being on vacation, you can spend 24/7 together, getting to know each other in ways that are not possible otherwise, enjoying the same activities together: water skiing, jet skiing, scuba diving, hiking, swimming, and so on. Would you choose 2 hours a day or 24 hours day? One day on a tropical island would equal one or two weeks of your stay in her country!
- You will have a chance to see how she behaves away from home. Being on her own will show you her ability to adjust to a different country, culture, and society.
- Being in a new setting can bring out qualities in your woman you wouldn't see at her home environment.
- You will save time. A trip to the Dominican Republic is a lot quicker than a visit to Russia, Ukraine, or Kazakhstan. Coming to Punta Cana will only take three hours of your time.
- You don't need to think about what to do and how to entertain your lady –

- A woman who has never been outside of her city might be uncomfortable in a new foreign setting. This might intensify if she doesn't speak the language.
- Women from some countries (for example, Belarus) might have to have a visa.
- You have no way to see her in her usual setting.
- You will not meet her family or friends which means you will be missing out on learning about important aspects of your woman's life.

tropical paradise and plenty of activities will take care of that for you. You will not run out of things to do.

- You will see a lot more of your woman than you would during a visit to her home country. Yes, I am talking about seeing her in a bikini, and no, I am not suggesting anything indecent. Every person relies on visual perception to determine their interest in the opposite sex. Being on a beach is a great way to test your chemistry and decide whether both of you like what you see. Imagine meeting the same woman in a fur coat – how well do you think you can determine attraction in this case?
- You do not need an entry visa.
- Your lady will most likely not require a visa to travel to the Caribbean.
- You will be in an English-speaking environment as most personnel and tourists will know the language.
- No police, no cops, anything goes – even drinking and driving.

Dating like a pro

Meeting your woman for the first time is a serious step. It is not something to be taken lightly, you must be prepared. Over the last few years I've asked some of my female clients to tell me what they would expect of a man visiting them and want to share this information with you.

***

While the entertainment industry today might be full of rugged hunks, they are good only for onscreen heroines. Real women will always prefer romance and courtesy, because no matter how emancipated or independent, every woman likes to be treated like a lady.

***

You must look good. Yes, I am talking about this again, after all, "Repetition is the mother of learning and the father of action, which makes it the architect of accomplishment." While there is no need for a tuxedo (unless, of course, you have planned an evening of opera and fancy dining), make sure that you dress up nicely. Coming in old jeans and a t-shirt is definitely not the way to win your lady's heart. First impressions are the most lasting ones, and you don't want to miss a chance to put your best foot forward. Depending on where you are going, you may have several options.

If you plan to go to a restaurant, a suit will be a great choice. However, if you are not comfortable wearing one, slacks and a shirt will also fit the occasion. For most people in Russia and CIS it is not very common to attend restaurants, so for them it is a special occasion. Also, Russian women tend to dress up more than women in Europe or US (especially when going out), so wearing more than casual clothes will also make you feel comfortable in your lady's presence. Going to a night club gives you more flexibility – jeans combined with a shirt or t-shirt will be a comfortable choice. If your first meeting is planned during the day in a café, hotel lobby or a coffee shop, wearing relaxed style clothing is acceptable. A good rule of thumb – when in doubt, don't go casual.

***

Your cologne matters. Women are more sensitive to smells than men. Don't use perfumes with a strong or sweet smell – you will make your date uncomfortable. Find something with a fresh, light smell.

***

You will be expected to pay for everything on your date, so make sure you exchange enough money before your meeting – cash is the preferred payment option in most FSU countries. Try to find out an approximate price range from someone you know (an agent, an interpreter, a hotel manager). The last thing you want to do is run around looking for an ATM or, worse, have to ask your date for money. It is also a good idea to settle the bill without much fuss – pay it while your lady steps out or excuse yourself and manage the issue. This is a good way to avoid awkward moments.

***

Keep a few questions ready in case the conversation gets slow. Don't ask things that require "yes" or "no" answers. Ask your woman something that would get her to open up and share more information about herself – i.e. Why do you like your job? What is your favorite childhood memory? What are some of your family traditions?

***

If you invite a lady to travel anywhere, within her country and outside its borders, it is your responsibility to pay her expenses.

***

Most people think that Russia and CIS countries are cold all year round. It is true only for the northern areas of Russia; most other areas will have regular four seasons. Spring and summer are the best time for a visit since you will be able to do things outdoors; many places in Russia and Ukraine will have plenty of options for swimming, camping and other similar activities. Winter is a great time if you want to experience the Russian cold or are interested in extreme sports (snowboarding, skiing). If your Russian friends or lady you are meeting share the same interests, it will be a great treat for them if you take them along, as many people living in Russia/Ukraine usually cannot afford such kind of vacation.

***

Things like toiletries, generic medicines, and food will be easily available in large cities; the further you travel in the country, the less choice you will have. In terms of clothes, make sure that you are dressed for the season. If you are traveling in winter, you will easily be able to buy most winter things in Russia (they will cost less than they would at home, too).

***

Plan your entire stay before you leave your home country as much as possible. Russian women don't like to be bossed around, but they like a man in charge – making plans will show you as a responsible individual and will be a welcome relief to Russian women, most of whom rarely get such a treat from the local men. On a subconscious level, careful planning will portray you as a reliable person who can take care of things, so a woman will feel more confident with you by her side. Tip: if you are visiting your lady at her home country, it is quite acceptable that you might not know what is available at her town for a date. In this case use the help of a dating agency professional or of a hotel manager/employee. Finding a dating agency is easy in Russia and other CIS countries, most agencies will help you arrange a date properly by suggesting restaurant and entertainment options. This service might be free or you might have to pay a small fee for their efforts.

***

Women love compliments. Make sure you compliment your date on the way she looks: you can talk about her dress, hair, smile, eyes, etc. If you are nervous and want to know you look all right, your Russian woman will feel the same – tripled. She can be just as nervous and need to know that you like the way she looks. Regardless of what you say, make sure you speak genuinely – women are very sensitive to lies, so if your Russian lady feels that you are hesitating, she might close up in thinking you are not sincere.

***

Bring flowers. It is common knowledge that bringing flowers for your date, pulling out her chair, opening a door or pouring wine are things gentlemen do – even though most men forget about it. Make sure that once the evening is over you walk your lady home or ensure a safe taxi ride for her (it is good manners to pay for the taxi ride as you arrange it for her). And don't worry that it will make you look old-fashioned – doing such things is nothing more than being considerate, and it is exactly what you want your woman to think about you.

Make sure you really listen to what your woman is saying. Nothing creates a worse impression than a distracted listener. If you are not paying attention to what your Russian woman says, you can be sure there will not be a second meeting – put yourself in her shoes, would you be impressed by someone who is not attentive to things you say? To avoid awkward silences and to make sure you are interested in what she says, ask her good questions to which you want to know the answers.

***

"Flaunt it, if you got it" is definitely not a good strategy to employ on your dates. While Russian women want to know that their man is established and financially secure, they will not appreciate you trying to impress her on purpose. It is best to avoid glorifying yourself, your success or status; otherwise a woman might feel like you are trying to buy her. However, tip a waiter well – women always pay attention to your generosity to others, especially people of service; be friendly with waiters, but take it down a notch when speaking to waitresses.

***

Follow up is good not only for job interviews, and a text message is not the way to do it. It is best to send her flowers with a note saying what a nice time you had and that you would like to see her again. If such option is not possible, it is okay to call her – your woman will appreciate the effort.

***

Think of her before you think about yourself. Being a gentleman is mainly about being considerate and thoughtful of others. If you are planning a meeting with your Russian lady, make sure that the plans will not be disruptive to your woman's schedule – take into consideration her work time, her living arrangements, and family situation. Consider her eating preferences: if you are planning a restaurant visit, make sure that you know in advance the type of food she likes – it would be really awkward if she were a vegetarian and you took her to a steak house.

***

Think outside the box. Movies and a restaurant are not the only options for a date. Take into account your lady's interests: if she likes art, plan a visit to an exhibition, if she is athletic – plan a hike or something of the sort. Whatever your ideas, make sure that there is enough "quiet" time so the two of you could talk and have time to get to know each other.

***

Renting a car in Russia/Ukraine is possible, but is not the best option; most roads are not very good and traffic rules can be very confusing, accepting bribes is still common among the traffic police, so you will be better off to leave driving to the natives.

***

You must have a visa to enter Russia and will have to register with Russian authorities upon arriving to the city of your stay. The visas are not too difficult to obtain, especially if you use a reliable travel agency. If you are staying in a hotel, they can handle the registration procedure for you.

***

Language is certainly an issue to consider. If you do not speak Russian, make sure that you have a reliable interpreter with you. You can easily find an interpreter to assist you in larger cities. It might be more problematic to find a skilled interpreter in smaller cities, and you certainly will not be able to find menus or signs in English.

***

If you move around on your own, it is a good idea to write down addresses of places you are going to, or have an electronic translator to be able to find your way and ask about the basics. Make sure that you have with you at all times the address of the place where you are staying to be able to get a taxi should you get lost.

***

Some people raise concerns that Russians are racist, but you will find just as much of this attitude in Russia as anywhere else. Remember that older generation of people was raised to consider everyone equal, and Russia maintained friendly relations with many other nations (India, China, etc.). It is true that some people might exhibit negative attitude towards Americans because of political views, but in no way will it put foreigners in danger, nor will anybody insult you if they find out you are from the United States.

***

It is highly unlikely that you will find as friendly cashiers and waiters as at home.

~ 109 ~

***

You will not be able to dial international numbers from street telephones.

***

Be prepared that your cell phone might not work in remote areas.

***

Finding a taxi will not be a problem. Even if you do not find a specially marked vehicle, you can easily hire any car – most drivers will be glad to give you a ride for a few extra rubles, but be certain to discuss the fee before you get in the car.

***

Russia has made some significant advances in technology, so you will not be cut off from the civilization – you can use internet in Internet cafés, post offices or hotels for fairly small fees, many public places now also offer Wi-Fi services.

***

Public transportation is widely available and cheap, but make sure that you know well which route to take and which direction you should go.

***

You can find that it is rather expensive to wash your clothes at the hotel, and some places can simply not have this service available. The easiest thing to do is to have a small pack of washing powder and wash your clothes yourself; you can hang them up to dry overnight in the bathroom, it will not be considered awkward or strange. Another alternative can be asking a cleaning lady to do so: if she or someone she knows will take care of your clothes for you, you can be certain that it will be cheaper and done well, besides, most hotel staff do not earn much and they will be happy to make some extra cash.

***

Food should not be of any concern. Most places, even smaller cities, will offer a wide range of food items – from national dishes to pizza. The only problem can be lack of English menus, so you might learn (write down) a few basic food items to make sure you can order.

~ 110 ~

Soups are very popular (especially famous Russian borsch) as well as dumplings with meat (pelmeni) or potatoes.

***

Quality of water will not be a problem as long as you use bottled water for drinking. Tap water can be of poor quality in some areas, so it is best not to drink it, but it safe to use for brushing teeth. When buying bottled water, pay attention to the type of water you are getting: when Russians refer to mineral water, they usually mean carbonated, slightly salty water, so if you want plain water, be sure to ask for non-salty, non-carbonated water.

***

Make sure that you bring electrical converters (electricity in Russia is 220 volt), the plugs in Russia are 2-pin thin of European standard.

***

If you are invited to visit someone, it is polite to bring a small gift with you (a box of candy, a bottle of wine, flowers).

***

You should try everything that your hosts offer you (even if it is just a small bite or a sip) – Russian people are very hospitable and when expecting company they will usually do their best to arrange a lot of food; if you refuse to eat they can get offended. If you make an attempt to skip something of what is being offered, you will soon find yourself exhausted of arguing, as your host will come up with a number of reasons why you should have it.

***

In case you are not sure how to handle certain situations, follow the lead of the natives. Whatever the situation, show respect for the Russian traditions and you will be able to enjoy numerous Russian traditions and country's immeasurable hospitality.

How to lose any Russian woman in 30 seconds

I have to share these two examples with you because I don't want you to repeat the same horrible mistakes the gentlemen in these stories made (all names have been changed, in case you are wondering).

Example # 1.

If John ever reads this book, he will immediately know that I am talking about him. John has been corresponding with Natasha, one of my female clients, for a while. They have not committed to each other, but have made plants to meet. They both attended a romantic tour I organized in the Dominican Republic. His lady arrived a day earlier and was excited about meeting the man she thought might become her future husband.

When the two met, they got along great. They spent an entire day together, hugging, kissing, smiling, and having a great time. In the evening the entire group of my guests gathered at the night club. After a few drinks everyone was having an even better time, laughing, dancing, and enjoying each other's company. At some point, John, having one hand on Natasha's knee and another around her shoulder, asked her in front of the other 15 people at the table if other women were available for dates. Needless to say, Natasha was stunned, speechless. What is worse, John didn't even understand what he did because the next moment he turned to me (I almost dropped my drink when I heard his question) and asked me if I could set up some dates for him for tomorrow because the woman whose knee he is rubbing doesn't seem to want to answer…

I think you can figure out what happened to him during the remainder of the trip – no woman wanted to talk to him, including his never-happened girlfriend. It's been five years since that instance, and he is still searching for the right girl. I guess, some people are just too curious and never quit "wondering".

Example # 2.

This happened during my Sacramento get-together. Larry (who, by the way, will also know that I am talking about him should he read this book) was one of the first to arrive to my dating party. He is a tall gentleman, a bit overweight, in his late 60's, well-groomed, well-established, and rather pleasant overall, despite his flashy golden watch and golden cufflinks. Knowing his situation, I wondered why he was still single. I didn't have to wait long to find out.

I greeted him at the time when he was speaking to two women in their fifties. I overheard him say that he is very serious in his search and is interested in finding a partner close to his age. I was so proud of him and thought he would be able to get engaged right away. Imagine my shock when, after I introduced myself, he turned to me brushing aside the two women he was just having a conversation with (he pushed one of them aside without apologizing) and exclaimed: "Wow, you are hot! This is the type of girl I want to marry. Are you available, Oksana?" (I was in my early 30's). I didn't know what to do with myself from the shame of the situation. Larry's complete disrespect for women, lying through his teeth, and being a complete jerk produced expected results – he didn't meet anyone that evening. In fact, every woman who has spoken to him that evening never wanted to speak to him again. I have spoken to him numerous times about respecting women and about being honest, but he is still searching and has not changed a bit. What is worse, he really thinks that he will find a decent woman.

As you see, these gentlemen are real "winners" in losing a woman in 30 seconds or less – but I am sure, you would not make such mistakes. However, this is not the only way things can go wrong when you are planning a meeting with your beautiful Russian bride. And since we are talking about logical, strategic planning of your trip to make it successful, let me share with you a few more situations where men make mistakes.

1. Buying airline tickets without proper research can be a waste. Several men I know bought tickets without checking the visa regime at their final destination; as a result, they were simply not allowed to board the connecting flight to reach their woman's country. They had to return to the USA – what a waste of time and money.
2. Some men do too much research – they go on the Internet, find horror stories about the country they plan to visit (which

generally happen to people who are not prepared for the trip) and give up the idea of visiting before they even start. The result: women with eyes full of tears in my overseas offices whose hopes to meet their potential partner were destroyed in the last minute.

3. Often men expect women and the environment overseas to be they are in their own home country. Lack of consideration for cultural differences often not only ruins a perfectly fine relationship, but also leaves women offended and disappointed.

4. Ego is one of the biggest hindrances to making a meeting in person successful. Some men expect a woman to fall in love with them the minute they meet because they... well, came all the way from America to meet her. Needless to say, such an attitude will never attract a woman. What is worse, men often suffer a huge blow to their self-esteem as a result of such meeting because Russian women are straightforward and will not keep quiet if they don't like something.

5. Of course, the worst possible thing that can happen is becoming a victim of a scam – I've seen men in my overseas offices completely desperate and crushed because they were taken advantage of, emotionally and financially, by vicious scam artists.

------------------------------ Resource! ------------------------------
Learn from the mistakes of scam victims in the bonus chapter at the end of the book and log on to www.oksanalove.com/rbscam to download a free chapter and a chance to win a free copy of my scam busting book "Scam me NOT".

There is a saying in Russian: "A man warned is a man armed" – now you know what can go wrong in planning a meeting with your Russian woman, which means that you will never repeat the same mistakes.

My Russian bride dumped me – what next?

It is natural that you expect your visit to be fun and exciting and return home with a beautiful woman as your fiancé. However, sometimes things can go differently than planned, and once you've met your Russian woman, you might hear that she is not interested in continuing the relationship.

The most obvious reason is that there is no chemistry. Sadly, you cannot do a thing to change this. As you already know, chemistry is something beyond our control; it is a natural physiological reaction of our body telling us if we are compatible with someone. The real trick here is to have her admit what she feels as soon as possible. Despite being straightforward, most Russian women won't know how to tell you they don't really feel any connection for fear of hurting your feelings. A woman will most likely wait until you return home and then send you an email telling you that she is not interested. Of course, this is ten times worse than her telling you about her lack of interest right away, but there is nothing you can do except watch for signs of her affection or lack thereof. What I have noticed with my female clients, they will often ask the agency to give the man the bad news if they don't feel any chemistry.

How you might know that she is not interested:

- She remains distant.
- You might feel like she is trying to avoid you by suddenly becoming busy and coming up with reasons why she cannot see you.
- She is not responding to physical contact – she does not return kisses, pulls her hands away when you try to hold them, and does not try to get close.
- Her body is always turned away from you during the conversation; she keeps her arms crossed on her chest, and maintains her distance.

While such an outcome is disappointing (I've seen many men very upset when women they came to meet didn't reciprocate), this is not the end of the world. First, you must realize that you could have done the same thing – imagine that you felt no interest in the woman after meeting her, what would you do? Second, you need to regroup and refocus as soon as possible. If you are overseas, it is a great opportunity to enjoy a different culture as well as meet some other

women in the vicinity – you might not leave with a fiancé, but at least you would have had a good time and you just might find someone you really like.

Remember that dating is about flexibility, fun, and meeting people until you find the right woman for you. I've met many men who, after realizing that nothing would transpire with the woman they wanted to meet, were able to

collect themselves and change their mindset to accept the possibility of meeting other women. In many cases these men ended up with the right woman in their lives. The key to making international dating work is to keep your options open and have your

pick form a pool of gorgeous women – not the other way around.

CHAPTER 9: PRACTICAL GUIDE TO VISITING YOUR RUSSIAN BRIDE

The real Russia

When you travel overseas, aside from meeting beautiful women, you will experience culture shock. I am certain of this because I've spoken with hundreds of my male clients who have visited Russia, Ukraine, and Kazakhstan – they didn't see bears on the streets, there was running water, but some other things definitely came as a shock. I would like to share these things with you, so that you know what to expect.

***

You will get a ten-year dose of second-hand smoke. While some restaurants and entertainment establishments are gradually introducing smoking and non-smoking sections, most places do not have such luxury. You will see bus drivers smoke as they perform their duties (with most of the smoke being blown inside the bus), people smoking on the bus stops and at the entry ways to buildings, sometimes even inside the buildings.

***

Dozens of taxi drivers will be standing right at the exit of an airport offering you their services, they might even start fighting as to who will give you a ride. If you show the slightest interest in their offer, they will follow you until you either get into your car or meet people waiting for you at the airport. Keep in mind that you will probably pay double if you choose to use services of taxi drivers at the airport.

***

There are three distinct groups of women in Russia – young women (or "devushkas"), middle-age women (or "zhenshiny"), and retired women (or "babushkas").

"Devushkas" Young Russian women are considered among the most beautiful in the world. You will find many tall, long-legged beauties walking the streets. The first thing you will notice is that their clothing is rather revealing and their hair and make-up is immaculate.

Many of them might seem overly confident, even arrogant, too blunt, and even pushy at times, but they will generally be quite different in relationships. Outward bravado is necessary to survive in everyday life in Russia, but it is considered almost unacceptable for a woman to make the first step in a relationship with a man. At the same time, they can easily push through a queue to get through it faster, argue with a police officer to get you out of a ticket, and drink vodka at par with men.

"Zhenshina" A typical portrait of a middle-aged Russian woman is that of an intelligent, well-educated woman, strongly devoted to her family. Such women will generally be less provoking in their appearance than younger women; however, it is not uncommon to see them wear short dresses, transparent tops, etc. Most such women either live in apartments with their parents or parents-in-law or at least manage two households to take care of the latter. While educated, many do not work in their field, nor earn much. After the collapse of the Soviet Union, many women of this age found it very difficult to make transition to a new way of life. Because of economic turmoil, many took jobs unrelated to their education or field of expertise, as long as it brought money to their household. Unless they are business women, they probably do not travel much, but in summer they are very likely to visit their family "dacha" (summer home). The main activities at such summer homes are growing vegetables, tending to the plot, with very little fun and relaxation.

Middle-aged women are usually the ones whom you will find most rude and gloomy. Most still apply Soviet mentality to communication and their work, without caring for customer service or being polite, because their wages do not change whether she smiles at you or yells at you. But whatever the task at hand, they will do their best to complete it, as they were taught to do things well, keep their reputation, and put commitment before family or personal interests.

"Babushka" Old women cannot go unnoticed if you ever visit Russia. They normally spend most of their time outdoors (on the benches in front of their apartment buildings), discussing latest news – from politics to their next door neighbor. Even at an old age, these women will surprise you with their stamina – they will easily do necessary shopping without any assistance, bargain, tell someone off, fight for a place on a bus, or boldly jump right to the front of the line. Most of these women have undergone hardships of war and they make a point of reminding others about it.

While physically capable, they will often take odd jobs to make some extra money, as state pays very low pensions (about $50-100/month). Typically, they live with their children since buying separate living quarters is very expensive. Often they practically replace kindergartens or nannies by helping to take care of grandchildren, while children's parents go to work. You will find many older women selling self-grown vegetables, jams and preserved vegetables (very common food in winter) or self-collected herbs in the markets as well as on the streets.

***

Bluntness and harshness seem to be distinctive Russian qualities, but the truth is, most of the time, they don't say things to offend anyone. Such bluntness can often be perceived as rude by people who come from nations that are used to more diplomatic communication and using hints to make a point, instead of saying things as they are. The only way to handle this is to learn not to take this personally and to do your best to understand the culture. If something seems out of hand to you, it is best to ask the person you are talking to what he/she means – it will help you both avoid misunderstandings.

***

When you will meet your woman for the first time, she might insist on having her own interpreter. In many cases, an interpreter will also be her friend. There is no need to feel intimidated by such a request – it is simply a way for her to feel comfortable in a setting with someone she has never met before.

***

Once you come in touch with Russians on a personal basis, you will see completely different people – welcoming, hospitable, and friendly. When you hear stories about Russian hospitality, you can be sure that they are true, as Russian hosts would give up their last piece of food to their guests. The best strategy to making the most of Russian people's hospitality is to have a little of each dish – many people who are not familiar with Russian traditions eat a lot of the salad or an appetizer and later find themselves incapable of eating the main course. If there are certain things you do not eat (i.e. if you are a vegetarian, allergic to certain foods, etc.), it is best to let your host know about it in advance; if you arrive and your host has cooked things that you will not eat, it will create an awfully awkward situation.

Gathering everyone at the table is a big affair. The meals normally include several courses and several types of drinks (alcoholic and regular – wine, vodka, cognac, juices, mineral water). Meals are usually followed by dessert: chocolates, cake, and fruit, served with tea or coffee.

While Russian cuisine is delicious, it can hold unexpected surprises. One story I heard firsthand is a good example. A group of Americans who traveled to Russia was invited to people's home. They were offered quite a few dishes, among them meat with a very unusual look and smell, which – one could tell – was presented by the hostess with pride. When the guests inquired what it was, they could barely hold in the food they had already eaten – it was cow tongue. In Russia it is considered a very special delicacy and is not cooked very often, generally for a fancy feast, so cooking it was a hosts way of showing her utmost respect and regard for the guests, while guests lost their appetite for the rest of the evening.

It is expected to have quite a few drinks on any Russian table, including vodka. You most likely will be forced to drink or at least try it, especially if you are in a house of your woman and she has older generation present there such as her parents or grandparents. You will hear word "davai" very often at the Russian table, which in this particular case means "Let's drink".

***

Friends are just as important to Russian people as their family and are, in fact, considered a part of the family by most people. It is not necessary to plan visits well in advance – friends and family can drop in any time or simply call before coming, and they will still be welcomed just the same.

***

If you get to observe your lady getting ready for work, this is what you will see: she will devote most of her time in the morning to making herself presentable with little time left for breakfast and last minute household tasks. Some women can take up to an hour and a half to get ready – this means doing their hair, makeup, selecting the proper outfit. Breakfast is a much less elaborate process – most people are satisfied with a sandwich and a cup of tea/coffee. As you will notice, most women in Russia always wear makeup and are dressed as if they are going out even if they are merely stepping out to grab something from a store.

***

Most people use public transportation (bus, trolleybus, tram, underground – where available) and have to travel from the outskirts of the city to the central areas. Generally, there are no vacant seats, and people are crammed in the vehicles like sardines. If you get to ride a bus, you are likely to be pushed, stepped on, and even yelled at, unless you are pregnant or with a small child – then someone might be kind enough to offer you a seat. During winter time, public transport is only a couple degrees warmer than the outdoors, so one not only faces inconvenience, but also gets cold while waiting and traveling.

***

Most women stop by a store after work on their way home. Most Russians shop as needed, instead of getting stocked up once a week, and most people select stores close to their home (usually within a couple miles walking distance). A woman who is not carrying many grocery bags is not a typical picture, it is more common to see women loaded with heavy bags after a work day than to see them reach home empty handed.

Most Russians still shop at the markets for food, clothes, and other items. To do so, one has to walk through rows of items, pushing others and getting pushed. Such a procedure usually takes several hours and most people I know reach home exhausted.

***

If you look around, you will see hundreds of girls wearing short skirts and heels. It is typical for the country, and therefore is not an indication of a girl being easy or anything of the sort. I remember when I first came to the US, I was excited when I found a pair of blood-red stilettos on sale (something I could not afford while living in Russia). I put them on once and never wore them again after my friends said only prostitutes wore such shoes – I had never heard of such nonsense and was really upset that my dream was ruined.

As you remember, there are more men than women, which is why women do their best to maintain as attractive appearance as possible. I am sure, sometimes it happens on a subconscious level, nevertheless, it's a fact. Just like desert plants have exceptionally bright and fragrant flowers to attract insects to pollinate them, so women always put their best foot forward through dressing attractively, looking appealing and well-groomed. As sad as it is, showing beauty before brains is sometimes the only way to be heard by a society based on chauvinistic principles and rules.

***

You will find many visitors from abroad; you will meet them in the night clubs, international upscale super markets, and restaurants.

***

In larger cities (above 300,000 population), you will see plenty of ATM machines. Remember that you will receive local currency; if you exchange money at the bank, you will have to pay a conversion fee + a transaction fee. Cash is the preferred method of payment. Credit card use is becoming more common. Most places will accept Visa and MasterCard, not too many places accept American express, and none will accept Discover. In smaller cities, you will have to look for ATM machines or exchange kiosks a bit harder. Make sure you keep enough cash for the weekend as banks and other financial establishments will be closed.

***

Taxi: most will charge based on mileage, hiring a driver for a day can cost from $15-20 per hour.

***

Apartments (which are called flats in Russia) are located in larger houses with multi levels, usually 4 per each floor. There is no ground floor, the numbering of building levels begins with "1".

***

If you plan to travel around the country, you will have several options: plane, train, bus or car. You will find regular flights to almost all major cities. You can buy tickets at travel agencies or at the train/bus station; some services will allow you to purchase tickets online, but it is rather uncommon.

Trains and buses are available for travel to all cities and even other countries, however, trains might not be the best option due to poor hygienic conditions. They will not be as nice as trains in Europe, for example, and you should be prepared to watch your luggage closely as stealing is still very common.

***

Language is an issue you should definitely consider. You will rarely be able to find an English-speaking person on the street outside of large cities, so if you do not feel confident of your Russian, it is best to have with you someone who speaks the language. If you do not know anyone who can accompany you, interpreters can be hired to assist you during your travel. You are also more likely to find English-speaking people in urban areas.

**

Drivers act rather unfriendly to each other; they cut each other off, get mad and curse quite often. In Russia, a driver is more important than a pedestrian, meaning that pedestrians need to watch out and be very attentive. Traffic Police members accept bribes, very often they will set situations up so they have a chance to make an extra buck. They will expect more money from foreigners.

**

Public toilets are not easy to find, you will have to pay a small fee to use them. Some of them can be plain toilet bowls next to each other without walls or doors between them, most of them will smell badly. You will see people use bushes as the toilet.

**

In order to use public phones, you will need coins or a card, you will not be able to dial international numbers from street telephones.

**

You will find many Internet cafés (rooms with a number of computers) which you can use to check your email or contact friends and family. Most of them are open late, some 24 hours. Many public places now also offer Wi-Fi services.

**

Prices will vary from place to place (depending on the size of the city, the type of an establishment you are visiting, etc.), but here is an approximate list of prices you can encounter:

Hotel/apartment for one person: $40 - 200 USD per day;
Interpreter: $100-200 per day;
Meals: $10-100 per meal;

Taxi: most will charge based on mileage, hiring a driver for a day can cost from $15-20 per hour;

Entertainment: cinema tickets – from $5, excursions – from $10, bowling/pool – from $20 per hour.

Gifts for your Russian bride

"We make a living by what we get. We make a life by what we give."

— Winston Churchill

Gift giving is quite common in Russia – most people will not even visit their friend's home without bringing a bottle of wine, a box or candy or some flowers. It is a sign of respect and affection for your host. It is expected even more from a gentleman who is courting a lady.

It is not a difficult thing to master. You must understand that gifts are not given to buy a woman's affection, it is a way for you to express your interest, to do something pleasant for your woman, and to express your appreciation. You don't have to wait for a holiday to give your woman a gift, it should come from your heart and make a statement "This is for you... just because."

The first thing you must remember is that gifts don't have to be excessively expensive. They are meant to be simply tokens of appreciation and something to remember you by. Of course, if you decide to give your woman diamonds every day, she certainly won't mind!

You can always use holidays of your woman's country as an excuse to give her presents, but you can also give them to congratulate her on an achievement (getting her diploma, finishing a project, etc.), to mark a major even in her life or simply to say "thank you" for her affection and time.

Let me share with you a story that illustrates my point. One of my private clients enrolled in my elite member program right before March 8, an International Women's Day, – a holiday widely celebrated in Russia and other former Soviet Union countries. He did some research and knew that it was one of the biggest holidays for women. Before he sent out a single email, he asked me to help him determine the best matches for him and on March 8 sent ten beautiful bouquets to ten beautiful women from "a mysterious admirer". Needless to say, all women were flattered and pleasantly surprised. This gentleman was almost 60, yet, every single woman he contacted was interested in meeting him even though they were in their 20's and 30's. Every woman was stunned by his attention and immediately realized that this gentleman was someone very unique. He introduced himself in an unusual way; with just a few clicks of a mouse button he achieved results most men spend months trying to achieve. Conclusion: an easy, quick, inexpensive gift can go a long way.

In all my years as a matchmaker, I've found that it is very difficult for men to grasp gift giving, so I would like to give you some ideas of appropriate gifts.

GIFTS BASED ON HOLIDAYS

HOLIDAY	SUGGESTED GIFT
January 1 – New Year	In fact, the celebration begins on December 31. Fruit baskets, champagne, sweets, ornaments, jewelry, and anything else you can think of will be a good fit for the occasion. This is the holiday of the most extensive gift giving, aside from a person's birthday or wedding.
January 7 – Russian Orthodox Christmas	Being winter time, most fruit is rather expensive. Consider giving a fruit/sweets basket. Your woman is not the only one who will appreciate such gift – her family, especially if she has children, will also enjoy it.
January 14 – Russian Old New Year	Champagne or wine with a box of chocolates is a great choice for the occasion.
February 14 –	You are safe with similar gifts as are

Valentine's day	common in your country – heart-shaped... anything: cake, candles, jewelry, candy.
March 8 – International Woman's Day	A bouquet of flowers is a MUST! It can be accompanied by other presents as well. In FSU countries, it is common to give flowers to every female member of the family.
April 20 (2014) - Easter	People usually give "paskha" to each other and exchange colored eggs. Giving a cake or sweets is a good idea.
Lady's B-day	This is the biggest occasion of the year. Flowers are a must, plus, a personal present – perfume, jewelry, book, etc.
B-day of a woman's child	If your woman has a child, you must know his/her B-day. Sweets, toys, fruit – all of these things are appropriate.

Make sure that you are sincere in your giving – women will feel that it comes from the heart and will appreciate even the smallest of gifts.

How to order presents

If you are using a dating agency to contact a woman overseas, you can use services of an agency to deliver a selected gift. In most cases they will take a photo of your lady with her gift.

Numerous gift delivery sites offer international services (FTD.com, Flowers.com). You will need to provide them with your woman's address and phone number to process your order. Most such companies are reliable and will also report back with a photo of the recipient with the gift.

You can always mail the gift yourself. It is the perfect option because in this case you are not limited in your gift selection. However, do not mail electronic items as they most likely will not clear customs, or your lady will have to pay tax on the package.

A great idea is to send her something from Victoria's Secret. Most women have heard of this shop, but its products are not available overseas. Anything goes: suites, jammies, perfume, make up, and even lingerie. However, word of caution regarding the last item: do not send such items unless you are very intimate with your woman or you know for certain that she will not be offended or uncomfortable when receiving such gift. You can generally make a fairly accurate deduction by looking at a woman's photos or videos – if they are very sexy and of erotic nature, it means a woman feels comfortable with her sexuality and will not freak out when she gets a set of beautiful lingerie.

Do NOT send women gift cards of any sorts – they will not be able to use them as most overseas shops are not available in Russia. It is also not a good idea to send iTunes gift cards because Russians usually get their music free.

Men often ask if it is appropriate to give presents to a woman's parents before having met the lady in person. Yes, it is, but only if you know for certain that she has spoken to her parents about you. If that is the case, a bouquet of flowers to her mother for her birthday, for a holiday, or just to make her acquaintance before meeting in person will be a pleasant surprise for your woman as well as her parents (and a bonus step to make a good impression on her family).

If you want to be certain about the gift you give to your woman, you can always test the waters to find out what she likes. You can ask her about general gift-giving traditions in her family and among her friends. You can also speak about "a friend" who is looking to give a gift to his Russian woman and ask for your lady's advice – it is unlikely that she will figure out that you are trying to surprise her with a gift.

More rules

Below you will find some rules about gift giving that are based on cultural traditions and common sense.

***

Never order an even number of flowers – in Russia even number of flowers is used to commemorate dead or to take to a funeral. Many international gift delivery companies will offer an arrangement of twelve roses – ask them to either add or remove one flower, or have the delivery person explain that it is an American tradition so that your lady doesn't freak out about getting a "dead person" bouquet.

***

Do not begin your acquaintance with food. I know a man who brought pasta, ketchup, and spam as a gift for him woman on their first date. The woman was quite angry and offended. After a few minutes she tried laughing at the situation wondering if she was too skinny for the man or if he wanted her to cook a meal for him. Needless to say, the relationship didn't go beyond the first meeting.

***

Do not give your lady clothes, unless you are shopping with her, know her size for certain, and know that she would definitely want a particular item. There are a few exceptions (I've mentioned some of them and will share a few more in a minute).

***

Candy, especially in cute boxes, is always a safe bet. Women love sweets, and pretty packaging will make it seem more special.

***

I suggest you think about bringing something for her child, if she has one. Cute tennis shoes, a t-shirt or a baseball hat from a well-known brand (i.e. Adidas, Nike) will be a hit. If you win your woman's child's heart, you will have more chances of winning her heart as well. If she has a small child, a toy or candy for children will also work well.

***

Men often bring t-shirts or baseball hats as gifts for women. While these are great practical souvenirs, be sure that you know the size of an item your woman would need: you don't want to give an XXL t-shirt to a lady of size 2 – this will make her feel like she is getting a one-fit-all kind of gift.

***

If you don't know your woman well, but are set on giving her a gift, go for the safe option – flowers, fruit or candy. Wine or champagne is okay, but only if you are certain she consumes alcohol.

***

If you know your lady fairly well, feel free to go for a more personal gift such as perfume. Most Russian women will enjoy branded perfume - Blv by Bvlgari, Chanel Chance or ACQUA DI GIOIA by Giorgio Armani. Most Victoria's Secret fragrances are accepted well. Most young women will enjoy a smell that is smooth, fresh, and not too sweet. MEXX woman or Jil Sander's "PURE" line are a great choice. It is a good idea to stay clear of sweet smells as it is not common for women to enjoy them. It is ideal if you know what perfume your lady uses or would like to have – in this case you will really be giving her a perfect gift.

***

Bringing small souvenirs from your home country is a great idea – something cultural as a small token of your affection will make a woman of your choice feel special and your gift unique. However, stay clear of items that say "Made in China".

***

If the woman you are coming to visit is trying to learn English, it might be a good idea to find something to help her do it (some books in simple language, software to help her study, etc.)

***

Do bring flowers to your first date.

***

Another perfect-and-always-suitable gift is a visit to a beauty salon. All women like to look good, but not all of them can find time or money to have someone else do their hair, nails, etc. Even if it's not the case, giving your girl an opportunity to get pampered will be a memorable event for her.

***

Whatever it is you bring, make sure it is light and unbreakable to avoid problems with luggage limits and handling.

***

Bring a few extra trinkets just in case you make some unexpected acquaintances and want to leave a souvenir for them.

***

When it comes to gifts, sky is the limit. Most women like a wide range of things (jewelry, accessories, collectibles, perfume), so you shouldn't have any difficulty figuring out what she would want.

***

If your meeting was successful, and you have decided to pursue your relationship, you should consider leaving something special for your Russian sweetheart before you leave the country. It can be a photo of you two, something special she will remember you by or simply something sweet you know she would like. A digital photo frame with loaded photos of you together is a great idea – she can keep the frame on her night stand where it will remind her of you every night.

When my fiancée was travelling back home after his first trip to Kazakhstan, I gave him a wrapped box and told him not to open it until he reached home. He promised he wouldn't, and when he opened the box, he found a small teddy bear sprayed with my perfume and a romantic note about the wonderful time we had. I knew it would take a long time to process all necessary documents, and I wanted him to feel my presence even if it is just my perfume. He later told me that the teddy bear remained on his night stand all the time, except times when he missed me the most – then it would stay on his pillow. He said that this teddy bear helped him to go through months of unbearable wait. This teddy bear was still sitting on his night stand, bearing the smell of my perfume, when I came to the USA several months later. Presents you give to your lady will do the same – they will remind her of you and make it easier to wait until you meet again.

How to impress the family of your Russian woman

When you find the perfect Russian woman, it is natural to want to do everything possible to keep your relationship positive and harmonious. As the two of you progress in your communication, it is important to remember that for most Russian ladies their family is a priority; and while you are not getting married to your lady's family, getting along with them is one of the keys to a happy life with your Russian bride in future.

Russian women are known for their family values; it is one of the main reasons many men decide to look for partners among them. Russian ladies are very loyal to their families; family comes first. Russian women make the most dedicated mothers and wives. Russian culture includes a lot of family time during holidays and everyday life, and your sweetheart will certainly place a lot of importance on her partner having a good relationship with her family.

To achieve this, you must show respect. Being kind, courteous, and following cultural customs are great ways to show your interest in becoming a part of the family. Be observant and pay attention to small family traditions (i.e. serving elders first at the table, etc.), then follow them. It will show your lady and her family that you are respectful and acknowledge their feelings.

It is also important to be thoughtful. Most Russian people are very hospitable and will treat you like a VIP, so you should be prepared to show your appreciation for such treatment. If you are invited to your Russian lady's family's home, remember not to come empty handed. You do not have to bring anything fancy, but having a small gift for the hosts will be a nice gesture. For example, you can bring flowers for the hostess and wine for the host, a dessert for everyone or something similar. Your effort will not go unnoticed; it will show your sweetheart's family that you thought about them in advance and prepared for the visit well.

Remember that actions speak louder than words. Your Russian lady's family will want to see your care and intentions for her, so whatever you tell your future in-laws, support it with actions. If you make a promise – keep it; do not promise things you cannot deliver. Seeing you be consistent in doing things you promise will help your Russian bride's family trust you and make them feel like their daughter will be in reliable hands.

Be honest with your bride's family. Be open about your intentions, describe how you see your future together, whether you plan to get married soon or would rather take things slow, and try to answer any other questions they may ask you. Since dating a man from abroad often means their daughter leaving for his country, many parents might be concerned about frequency of communication and being able to keep in touch. Try to address any concerns they might have or even look for a compromise together. Your lady's parents and family will appreciate you being upfront and honest about the future possibilities; it will help them adjust their expectations and will result in less tension for everyone.

Once you and your Russian lady have made plans to join your lives in future, take any opportunity you can to communicate with her family. This can be especially useful when you visit your sweetheart's country. Make a point of spending time with her family and getting to know each other. Tell them about your life, ask about theirs – such communication will help your lady's parents be more accepting of you and can also help you learn more about your sweetheart: knowing her family history can explain a lot of who she is.

Whatever steps you take to getting to know you Russian woman's family, make sure that you are genuine. Having your bride's family accept you and know who you are will be a great way to ensure a happy future for you and your sweetheart. Keeping a warm and friendly relationship with your in-laws is important because they always have a huge impact on your girl's decisions (as I've said numerous times, Russian women are very close to their families). The secret to keeping an excellent relationship with your in-laws is to make their daughter happy. It is that simple. Every parent will be the happiest person in the world if their child is happy. Make your in-laws realize that they are not losing their daughter, but that they are gaining a true and loving son (you!).

Observing the dynamics of her family. (modern Russian women)

Russian women have always been the stronger ones in the family, even though men have a bigger ego and usually earn money. Most Russian men are chauvinistic and honestly believe that men are superior to women. This has always been stressed in the Russian society, but in reality, women are usually the ones holding families together as well as the society. Men might be earning the money in the family, but women normally decide how to spend it on family needs. Women are usually the ones who handle most organizational issues – budget, taking care of the apartment (sure, men may be driving the nails into the walls, but women are the ones who tell them where to do it!), taking care of children, and managing family matters.

Partially, the reason for this is that after WWI and WWII there simply were not enough men to do everything that was required (most men died during the war, were crippled, emotionally devastated, often incapable of working, and so on), so women were the ones who had to revive the country and their homes. Finding a decent (read: not a mental or physical cripple, able to work) man was all women wanted to create families, and that has shaped the way Russian women approach life even today.

Since Russian women have not had a chance to get used to men being the stronger ones in the society and the family, they have slowly accepted the fact that men are fairly "helpless" and stopped trying to change this. It is common to hear women say that men are big children and should be treated as such – you will find that women often serve dinner to their men, cook and care for them even in little things, despite the fact that men are perfectly capable to make a sandwich or warm up dinner on their own!! This attitude slowly expanded into other areas of life, and women have become more proactive in their life and careers. With the economic crisis booming, it is pretty common to hear stories about men who have lost their jobs and haven't been able to find new employment, thus placing the burden of providing for the family on women's shoulders. Men will often say that they cannot find a worthy job, meaning that a computer technicians will not work as a part-time clerk at a hardware store even he has been out of a job for six months – he would consider this an insult to his dignity, even if it means passing up extra income for the family! Yet, women will do whatever it takes to earn enough to make sure the family is taken care of – they will be prepared to work several jobs and will not think that cleaning toilets is beneath their dignity if it means that their children will be fed and dressed.

Having seen this childhood, many young Russian women are now changing their attitude to either manipulating men or choosing to be alone to avoid such relationships. You will find more young women focused on their careers, education, and self-improvement, instead of selecting a much less attractive option of being a servant to a man.

When you are at your woman's home meeting her parents and siblings, I suggest that you observe the dynamics of her family carefully. Watch how men of the family are treated. It is possible that an older brother will be the man of the family, if a father and a grandfather are deceased or not present. Observe everything: how other family members speak to men, whether they listen to them, how they are treated, how the man of the family is perceived, whether he is respected and whether his word carries any clout in making decisions. Take notice of how your Russian bride speaks of her father, grandfather, older brother or any other man who has had a major impact on her life.

You need to pay attention to these things because they will affect your relationship with the woman – the way she treats men in her family is exactly the way she will treat you, and it will not make any difference that you are a completely different person and are nothing like men in her family. If you notice that men are not being taken seriously, and women are the ones making all the important decisions, you can certainly expect to be bossed around and have a few issues over authority within the family. If you see that men are treated as authority and with great respect, you can be sure that you will be given the same treatment and will be expected to display similar qualities.

These things might seem obvious, but many foreign men completely ignore this important step because they are in love. At that point, they only care about being with their future wife, making a good impression on her family, and, hopefully, forgetting all about them once she has moved abroad. Most men completely overlook the relationship dynamics in their future wife's biological family, forgetting that her habits and what she has observed for years between her mother and father, for example, has already left an indelible imprint in her mind and will manifest in her own marriage.

If something about the way men are treated in the family concerns you, you should find a tactful way to discuss this with your potential bride and express your concerns and views on family life and relationships between men and women (not in front of her family, of course!). If you want to gain respect of your future wife's family, it is important to show confidence in yourself and in your future with your Russian woman by sharing concrete plans and ideas about your future family, as well as show respect to both her parents, regardless of who plays the dominant role in her family.

Internet access

It will be important for you to keep in touch with your family and friends during your visit. There are several Internet options available: you can use Wi-Fi wireless internet, mobile internet access, internet cafes, ADSL broadband and LAN, dial-up internet access.

Wi-Fi technology was not widely spread in Russia and Ukraine a short while back. Much has changed in the recent years, and now you can find Wi-Fi connection at most public places. This option is attractive for those who travel with their own computer. In order to take advantage of this opportunity, you need to have a wireless network card installed in your laptop. Most modern laptops will have them included; if not, you can buy such a card for about $50-100 dollars at most computer stores. You can find Wi-Fi spots in supermarkets, cafes and restaurants, railway stations/airports, night clubs, and hotels. Most of the time this service is free, some can charge up to $5-10 per hour. If you are traveling to less prominent cities, check Wi-Fi availability prior to traveling.

Mobile internet is a fairly popular option of access in Russia and Ukraine (they use GPRS and 3G networks). GPRS internet access offers speed up to 56 kB/s, it is fairly cheap, so your best bet is to get a Russian phone card – you will save a lot of money on roaming charges. Most large networks will be easily available in most locations. In Russia, for example, such companies as MTS, BeeLine, and Megafon are the most popular choices; MTS and BeeLine are also available in Ukraine, along with Kyivstar and Life. MTS has also launched 4G networks in Russia and Ukraine. While limited, the phone company is constantly expanding opportunities for this type of access.

If you are traveling without a laptop, you might find use of Internet cafés the most suitable option. Many of them are open 24 hours a day; they also offer a wide range of services (scanning, printing, saving data, business conferences, etc.) and have a wide range of software installed and ready to use. The cost of their services ranges between $1-2/hour. It is not a problem to find them in large cities; however, it might be more challenging to find them in smaller cities. Ask your hotel clerk or one of the locals to help you find them if you encounter any difficulties.

If you are staying in Russia or Ukraine for a long time, you might consider using a high-speed internet service, available through LAN (local area networks) and ADSL providers. This service will be available in most large to medium cities. You will need to place a request with a local cable company; they will usually set everything up within a couple of weeks. The price for setting up such service ranges between $20-60, a monthly fee will run between $15-$50/per month, depending on the speed and number of computers you will need to connect. You can easily have a 1Gb traffic with 512 kB/s speed for $30-40/per month. In case you need more speed, LAN providers can set up Ethernet cable in your apartment; this will cost more than ADSL, you will also require Ethernet card installed in your computer.

Dial-up is widely available; however, this option is being used less and less frequently. Many phone companies will have a contract-free option, where you can pay per time used; the set up is also easy – you will need an extra phone cable and a modem. However, be prepared that the lines will be busy and you will have to attempt connection several times. Phone companies usually provide detailed instructions for getting connected.

Most large networks and telecom companies have websites with all necessary information available. If you contact their headquarters, you will, probably, find English-speaking representatives to help you answer any questions you might have.

Money: information, costs, safety

You already have an idea about some approximate costs you can encounter during your trip, but I feel the subject of money cannot be discussed enough. Naturally, one of the most important aspects of traveling abroad is dealing with foreign currency and knowing how to manage your money while overseas. In most CIS countries, US dollar and Euro are the most common circulating currencies. Be sure to check recent exchange rates on the Internet before you leave.

You will have to use local currency as most places will not accept dollars or Euro, but you can easily exchange such currency in banks or exchange terminals. When it comes to private cash transactions (for example, paying your interpreter), you might be able to use US dollar or Euro.

Airports, hotels, and railway stations are the most tempting places to exchange money once you reach the country. However, they usually offer the worst rates, so only exchange a minimum amount. Banks, of course, are the most reliable source for currency exchange, and it is best to avoid using outdoor exchange kiosks. Keep in mind that some places (even some banks) may refuse to accept old/worn bills; make sure that you bring notes that are in good condition.

You should, no doubt, have some cash while traveling - $300-500 should be enough for initial expenses (transportation, hotel, food). If you plan to bring larger amount of cash, you should also remember that there is a limit on the amount of cash you bring into the country; generally, amount over $10 000 USD must be declared upon entering the country. It is best to keep money as credit cards or traveler's cheques (the most secure option). Cheques are attractive because you are the only one who can use them, they can be reissued if lost (as long as you write down their numbers in advance), but be prepared to pay a commission on cashing and refunding the cheques. It is also important to remember that you will not be able to pay with traveler's cheques in shops, restaurants or hotels; you can only cash them in at banks.

Credit cards allow you to keep track of all expenses through receipts; you can always cancel the card in case it is lost or stolen. Large cities have many cash machines where you can use credit cards to withdraw cash – big hotels and banks are the best option for this; many shops and restaurants will also accept select cards (Visa and MasterCard are accepted most frequently, Discover and Amex are almost never accepted). It might be a problem to exchange cheques or cash in cards in smaller towns, so it is best to use cash if you are traveling outside big cities.

When taking cash out of ATM, be prepared that your bank will charge you a currency conversion fee + your bank's transaction fee (about 5$ per transaction regardless the amount) + you will be charged a transaction fee by the bank that ATM machine belongs to. You will be receiving the currency of the country you are in; it will not be dollars or euros (the reason for a currency conversion fee from your bank, which is normally about 1% of the amount). I know that many banks can wave the currency conversion fee if you call them upon your return back home and ask them nicely to refund those fees. Banks will not refund transaction fees.

If you are using credit cards to pay for things while overseas, your credit card company will be charging you currency conversion fee as well. You can ask them to wave it as well. If you are collecting miles or reward points with your credit cards, then of course you should use them to pay for things while overseas. If you are not enrolled in any reward programs, you should – you will be pleasantly surprised at what you can get back in terms of money back options, travel miles, and other rewards. There are plenty of credit card companies that will offer you many bonuses for opening a credit card with them; for example, you can receive a bonus of 30,000 – 50,000 flight miles on American Airlines, which equals to 1 or 2 round trip tickets to the USA, or $200 - $500 money back after you spend $1000 - $2000 on your card. Plus, when you are using your credit card overseas, it gives you extra protection vs. spending cash. A credit card, if stolen, can be cancelled, and you are not responsible for the charges. But if your wallet with cash is stolen, you will never see it again.

There are a few precautions one should take regarding money when traveling abroad. As mentioned, you should write down numbers of your traveler's cheques, cards, and emergency numbers which you can call to block expenditures if anything is lost or stolen. It is also a good idea to keep your money in different forms: keep some of it in cash, some in traveler's cheques, and some in credit cards. You should also consider keeping money in different places (wallet, suitcase, laptop bag) – you will have a backup in case of theft or problem.

If you lose money or have it stolen and have no reserved stash to rely on, you can easily have someone transfer money to you. There are many services available for money transfer: Western Union, MoneyGram, etc. In case you are out of options, you can also turn to the embassy of your country for help – they will be able to offer necessary resources to handle any problems.

Prices will vary from place to place (depending on the size of the city, the type of establishment you are visiting, etc.), but you can have an approximate idea of what to expect:

	Ukraine		Russia		Kazakhstan	
	Small city	Large city	Small city	Large city	Small city	Large city
Hotel / apartment, 4 star	$30	$120	$40	$200 +	$50	$100 +
Meals, 4 star restaurant	$5 - 10	$20-$30	$20	$50 +	$25	$50+
Taxi within city: across town	$5 - 10	$30	$30	$100	$15	$40

Taxi: daily rate	$50+	$80 +	$50 +	$150+	$50 +	$80 +
Entertainment: cinema tickets	from $5	from $10	from $5	from $10	from $5	from $10
Entertainment: excursions	from $10	from $30	from $20	from $40	from $20	from $40
Entertainment: bowling/pool per hour	from $10	from $20	from $20	from $30	from $15	from $20

Keep in mind other expenses you will encounter: unless arranged in advance, you will need to pay agencies for introduction of the ladies (if you are planning to use an agency); you may want to buy a gift or flowers when going on a date with a lady you are meeting; if you are arranging a meeting with a lady outside of her home city, you should be ready to pay for her transportation and stay.

Apartment vs. hotels

When planning your trip, you will most likely be offered a choice between a hotel and an apartment for your stay. Obviously, hotels are a more common choice. Depending on the size of a hotel, starting price can range from $15-200+/night. Naturally, it is up to you, but apartments are a much better value for your money, especially if you are planning to stay somewhere for a long time. Prices for such apartments will vary from $30/night up to $100/night; if you are renting them long-term, some landlords might be ready to discuss discounts. Hotels generally have poor service with very few commodities (except expensive places) and give you no privacy. Most apartments are furnished well; they will have everything for a comfortable stay (TV, internet access, phone) and will be located within walking distance of stores, transportation, and central city areas.

Emergency during travel – when you should panic

Basically, never. Traveling to former USSR countries can be an unusual experience in itself, especially if you are visiting the country for the first time. But it is highly unlikely that you will encounter any situation in which panic will be justified.

LOSING PASSPORT AND YOUR VISA (if required)

- Make sure you always keep these documents in a secure spot (inner jacket pocket, money belt, etc.).
- Do not leave these documents in the hotel room when you leave; do not show them to strangers out of curiosity; if you do, make sure they always remain in your sight.
- Keep a notarized copy of your passport and visa – this will be helpful if you lose the documents.
- If you lose your passport, the most important thing to do is not to panic!
- Visit the nearest police station right away to get an official confirmation that your passport was lost.
- Have your return ticket or a printed confirmation of booking on hand.
- Contact your embassy immediately after you discover that you lost documents. The embassy is also the place where you will need to turn to for restoring your visa and passport. Information about embassies abroad can easily be found on the Internet.
- In case you need to have passport photos done, you can turn to any photo studio. Many such places offer express services – for a slightly larger fee you can have the photos ready within 20 minutes. Such photo studios are not difficult to find, and virtually all of them will be able to take your photograph for a passport.
- Keep a copy of an invitation letter or documentation from your tour agency, having this document will make it easier to restore your visa.
- Take all your documents to the office which provided your visa support (introduction agency, tour agency). You will need to pay the fine of about $150 to immigration and, given there are no complications, can receive a new visa within a week.

Attention: these procedures are valid for Russia. Other CIS countries might have slightly different requirements. Know how to contact your embassy; consult them immediately in case of an emergency.

RIP OFF BY CUSTOMS

Many foreigners have been taken advantage of by customs. Customs officers try to get money from foreigners by delaying them and claiming there are problems. However, such situations are becoming less common. Recently Russian parliament introduced a law which eliminated such problems. However, to be on the safe side, you should check custom regulations prior to travel. By law, one can bring up to $3000 US in cash (or equivalent) into Russia without declaring the sum (this means you do not have to fill out the customs declaration form and can proceed through the green corridor). If you carry a larger sum of money, you must fill out customs declaration form and declare available cash when leaving Russia. Large international airports also have customs information counters where you can resolve any issues.

LOST CREDIT CARD

Contact the credit card company immediately so they can block your card. You can also contact your bank and ask them to issue a new card. Information about credit card centers in the city you are visiting can be found on the Internet. It is a good idea to have this information on hand prior to traveling, so you do not waste any time.

NO LIVING ARRANGEMENTS

If you have arrived without planned living arrangements, the easiest thing to do is to go to the largest hotel in the area. Large hotels are likely to have vacancies and are easy to find in directories or online. If they do not have vacancies, ask them to recommend something. If you still have not been able to find anything, try yellow pages on your own or ask for help from taxi drivers – they usually have information about smaller hotels or private apartments for rent. In large/popular cities, you may find landlords at the train stations or in airports offering apartments for rent; of course, this should be used as the last resort measure, from a safety standpoint.

If you've exhausted all resources and still don't have a place to stay, you can always spend some time at the train station/airport where paid resort lounges are available. If you do not need sleep and feel like going for a walk or spending some time at an Internet café, you can leave your luggage at a locker in the airport or at the train station.

GOING INTO POLICE CUSTODY

Normally, police in Russia and neighboring countries will not create problems unless you've done something really naughty. However, even if they are wrong, the key to handling such a situation is to keep your cool and show them you know your rights (make sure you get some information about this in advance). Avoid getting haughty with the police; the best thing to do is to calmly let them know you are willing to work out the situation.

In Russia, for example, you cannot be detained for more than 3 hours if the police suspect you were involved in a crime, unless they have trouble identifying your persona (i.e. if you don't have proper documents) or have established that you really committed a crime. Even after it is proven that you were involved in a crime, you cannot be detained for more than 24 hours. One can be arrested (but detained no longer than 15 days) if a crime is more serious; but this also cannot be done without a decree from a judge.

Among the most common penalties are:

- Not having a visa registration (applicable to Russia);
- Disturbing public order (being drunk, cursing the police, inappropriate sexual behavior in public, etc.);
- Drinking alcohol in public (alcoholic drinks are considered those containing over 12% of alcohol; beer is not one of them);
- Carrying drugs.

Of course, Russian police members are well-known for taking bribes, so your best protection is to know the rules or at least look like you know what you are talking about so they do not intimidate you.

Health and safety advice

There are many myths surrounding health and safety situation in Russia. Some Americans I've known brought their own food with them and nearly starved themselves for fear of drinking and eating anything. However, generally, Russia and Ukraine are no more dangerous than any other European country in terms of health risks, and you do not need to take any particular precautions before traveling.

You will be perfectly fine with a few basic rules to follow regarding food and water.

- Make sure that you always wash fruit and vegetables before eating, especially if you are buying them from the market – some farms use pesticides or fertilizers that are sprayed over the crops.
- Keep your hands clean – you might not always find a wash room, so hygienic liquids and napkins will come in handy. It may seem like these are very obvious things, but they are important to remember because most problems come precisely because of negligence in such simple rules of hygiene.
- You should also be careful with water. While safe to brush your teeth and wash your dishes, tap water is not recommended for drinking. It is most commonly disinfected with chlorine and other chemicals, so it is best if you use filters, boil water or drink bottled water.

You do not require any vaccinations upon entry to Russia/Ukraine. In Russia, however, you might need to have an AIDS certificate on hand before you can receive your visa. The embassy is not enforcing it, as far as I know. Ukraine does not have any demands in terms of vaccinations, but the situation with AIDS is quite disturbing: the HIV/AIDS epidemic in Ukraine is one of the fastest growing in the world.

Other venereal diseases are also very common, so be sure that you always use condoms and are selective in partners you choose. Personal hygiene products are easily available in most stores and pharmacies. Generic medicines (aspirin, vitamins, bandages) are readily available, including products of international brands. If you are taking any particular medication, it is best that you take with you enough of it for the duration of your travel. If by some chance you do require a refill while abroad, make sure you know the Latin name of a particular medicine. Certain medicines (i.e. narcotic, psychotropic) can fall under restrictions for bringing them into the countries you visit, so make sure you have your prescription with you. It is a good idea to check with customs the requirements for such items prior to traveling.

Health system in CIS countries is very different from what is common in Europe and the US. It is funded by the state, and since the budget is very small, most hospitals are in poor condition and clinics generally have long queues. If you want medical healthcare of higher standards, it is best to turn to private clinics which are becoming more popular. Their services will be fairly expensive, but cheaper than what you'd expect in your home country. If you know someone in the country you are visiting, ask them to suggest a doctor to visit – this can be a cheaper and a more reliable option. Some CIS countries will require health insurance (like Russia, for example), while others do not demand any insurance coverage.

General rules

Some stereotypes portray Russia as full of mafia and troublemakers, but it is not any more dangerous to travel there than to any other European country, especially if you follow common travel safety rules. Some obvious suggestions are:

- Make a copy of all your travel documents and keep it in a safe place. It is helpful to keep on hand emergency phone numbers and contacts (embassy, credit card information, etc).

- Keep your money in a safe place (i.e. money belt, special bag) and do not carry all of it with you at once. Keep it divided to cash, cards, cheques. Do not flaunt cash you have in public.

- Avoid dark places and walking in unfamiliar places at night.

- Avoid getting into arguments with local police and people who look suspicious, but at the same time do not be afraid. If you speak to police, be confident and let them know you want to settle matters peacefully and are not looking for trouble.

- Should any emergency happen (i.e. losing your documents, having something stolen), turn to police or authorities immediately in order to have a written confirmation of the problem. This notice will help you take care of the problem once you turn to your embassy (or other authorities) for help.

Naturally, staying in large cities, you will be more likely to find all necessary things you might require. Small towns and villages will not have much choice. Different regions might have small differences (i.e. in some places you pay for using public transportation upon entering the bus, while in others – upon exiting).

It is always a good idea to talk to people who have already traveled to the places you plan to visit (Internet forums are a great resource), and, of course, talk to your sweetheart about any concerns you have – she will certainly be glad to share the information and even help you with some things.

Travel checklist

Things to do before departure:

- Book an apartment or a hotel;
- Check visa requirements and get an entry visa if needed;
- Arrange transportation (pick up at the airport);
- Notify an interpreter of travel dates;
- Find up to three emergency contacts overseas (your woman, friends, agency representatives);
- Make 3 copies of your passport and visa and keep them in 3 separate places. It is ideal to have the copies notarized;
- Call the phone company to activate international calling feature;
- Call credit card companies and notify them of travel times to ensure they don't block accounts;

- Check and print names of restaurants, art galleries, exhibitions, theaters, things to do in the place you will visit (Internet is a good resource);
- Make a list of souvenirs to take overseas, make a list of gifts to bring home;
- Check wardrobe, prepare clothes to be warn, do additional shopping if required;
- Check all ATM pin numbers to make sure they work;
- Make a list of credit card companies and their customer support numbers;
- Get a haircut;
- Shave off moustache and beard;
- Clean and polish dress shoes;
- Make a trip to the bank to get notes in good condition;
- Write down contacts of a travel agency in the city abroad;
- Make a written list of important numbers for friends/family in case phone or computer get stolen or lost;
- Write down numbers of traveler's cheques, cards, and emergency numbers;
- Find a light suitcase to minimize luggage weight.

Seasonal travel: what to bring in summer

- Bathing suit (swimming shorts);
- Sunscreen lotion, bug repellant;
- Sunglasses:
- Baseball hat;
- Sweater (for cooler nights) – you can always offer it to your lady when she gets cold.

Seasonal travel: what to bring in winter

- Warm jacket;
- Warm hat;
- Warm woolen socks;
- Thermal underclothes;
- Warm gloves.

Things to pack

- Passport, valid for six months after the planned date of travel;
- Three copies of passport;
- Driver's license in case you decide to drive or rent a car;
- Entertainment for travel;
- Dictionary (electronic or regular);
- Pen and paper;
- Travel pillow for the flight;
- Laptop;
- Chargers and converters;
- Photo or video camera;
- Suit or tuxedo if you plan to go to an opera or attend a similar event;
- Dress shirts (2) + tie + dress shoes;
- Clean, washed, ironed clothes (make sure nothing is torn and everything is in a perfect condition);
- Night club clothes – modern jeans and a stylish shirt or t-shirt;
- Comfortable shoes for walking;
- Tennis shoes, sport suit, socks;
- Souvenirs;
- Toiletries decanted into small bottles;
- Chewing gum, mouth wash, toothpaste, toothbrush, and lip balm;
- Small medicine set (Alka-Seltzer, aspirin, Pepto-Bismol, band aid, basic cold medicine, allergy medicine);
- Good cologne (something like Channel Egoiste, Givenchy Blue, Lacoste);
- Razor + shaving cream + after shave, hair brush, hair products if you use any;
- Small pack of washing powder to wash clothes if you plan to do it yourself;
- A small pack of hygienic liquids or wet napkins;
- Gifts for your woman, her family;
- A bottle of wine in case your Russian woman decides to spend a few hours with you after picking you up at the airport (if you get in at the middle of the night, you might not find an open shop);

- Prescription medicine if you are using any, make sure you have your prescription or a letter from your doctor as well;
- Digital photo frame so you can load photos from the trip and give to your sweetheart before you leave;
- Travel cheques, credit cards, cash (divide between several spots);
- Engagement ring or promise ring for when things go the way you want them to;
- Printed kit of fiancée visa paperwork (we will talk about it in the next chapter).

Additional things to pack, if you have room left:
- Candles for a romantic dinner in your apartment or romantic time together;
- Mini-speakers to connect to your phone or computer;
- Scented massage oil (coconut oil is the best) for the time when you get cozy with your sweetheart.

This should be enough to have you ready for anything that might come your way while you are overseas. Wonderful things are just around the corner – the woman of your dreams is almost in your arms!

CHAPTER 10: BRINGING YOUR RUSSIAN BRIDE HOME

Why Russian women don't travel abroad to find a husband

Men often wonder why not too many Russian women travel abroad or move to a different country if they want to marry a foreigner. There is a host of reasons for this, and it is my pleasure to share with you most common of them.

Money. Rather, lack of it. Wages are not very high in former Soviet countries, travel expenses are a luxury rather than a necessity. Most women earn between $200-300 a month and put large sums of money towards the family budget; the cost of tickets to the US is between $1300-2000 – as you understand, a Russian woman will have to save for a long time before she would be able to afford the airfare, not to mention other expenses.

Visas. Citizens of FSU countries are limited in their travel by having to obtain visas and various permissions before entering foreign countries. To obtain a visa, they must submit a packet of documents (proof of income, personal data, etc.) to the embassy of the country they wish to visit; the embassy will review the application (normally within 2-4 weeks) and grant/deny a visa which will allow the applicant to enter a particular country. Visas can be of different types (tourist, business, student, non-immigrant, immigrant) and can be valid for different periods, from several weeks to several years. Permanent visas, which would allow a woman to live in a particular country, are a lot harder to obtain, take longer to process, and require many documents. Embassies are generally reluctant to issue visas to young, single women for fear they might meet someone abroad and attempt to stay in the country by getting married. United States of America and European countries have the highest decline rate when it comes to issuing tourist, business, and student visas to single women.

Social issues. Moving to a foreign country is a big step which is hard enough to handle even for couples – women who move abroad to live with their husbands, even the most supportive ones, face many difficulties while adapting to a new culture and a different society. It is twice the stress for a single woman: she has to quit her job, leave her family and friends, face a number of difficulties, and build her life from scratch.

Knowing this, you can surely appreciate Russian women who are already living in the USA – they would have overcome a number of obstacles to re-establish their life in a new environment. Now you know that these women are natural achievers and make things happen, you can be certain that they will not quit when things get tough. Such women are also more likely to be easily adaptable and can cope with change; they generally have an entrepreneurial mind and can become successful in business.

Bringing your Russian bride home: visa options

Now is the time to talk about what you need to do to bring your Russian bride into your country. This is a bit boring, but very important. You have several options when it comes to marrying your sweetheart.

Scenario # 1. She comes on a student visa; you get married while she is in the country.

Scenario # 2. You first meet outside of your country, then bring her on a fiancé visa to get married.

Scenario # 3. She comes on a tourist visa; you get married while she is in the country.

Scenario # 4. She is already in your country on a valid visa when you decide to marry her.

In every case the process will be different.

However, whatever you do, do not marry your bride in her country because it will take you two-three years longer to process a visa for a wife. It used to be a lot quicker – you could get the whole thing completed in a matter of months (engagement, marriage, filing documents, and receiving a visa). Now it can take up to three years to bring your wife into your country – I speak based on observations of struggles some couples go through during this extensive, time consuming process.

Scenario # 1. She comes on a student visa; you get married while she is in the country.

You must realize that bringing your wife into your country on a student visa is the most expensive option, but the one with the least amount of paperwork. Still, there are challenges to deal with: your wife has to be accepted by a university which must issue a form stating that she is officially accepted to study. You (or your bride) will have to present proof of having sufficient funds to pay for the schooling.

Once a student arrives to the university, she will HAVE TO ATTEND the university and maintain a certain grade point average. In case she doesn't, the university has the right to revoke the official confirmation of her student status which means she will have to leave the country. Immigration is automatically alerted once the student status confirmation is cancelled. On average, you will have to spend about $15,000/year. You can marry your Russian bride while she studies and apply for adjustment of status (green card application).

Enrolling your lady into English study programs might be the most beneficial option, as she will have a chance to improve her language skills as well as marry you. Once married, you can file for adjustment of status (green card application). However, such programs last only a few months, she will still have to attend classes and return home once the study program is over.

Please, note: visas for students and exchange students are very different. You may not marry an exchange student.

Scenario # 2. You first meet outside of your country, then bring her on a fiancé visa to get married.

For this option, you can meet your bride in her country or on a neutral territory; after you've met, you can apply for a fiancé visa and marry her once she arrives to your country. In this case, you must be prepared to wait. It may take six months to a year from the time you meet and file a fiancé visa application until she receives a visa. Ukraine and Belarus may take longer.

Both of you must also be ready to deal with a lot of paperwork (proof of income, divorce papers, if applicable, medical records, history of your correspondence, and much more). Once you have submitted the packet of documents, your lady will receive a notification about the time for an interview at your country's embassy. During the interview, the embassy employee will decide whether to grant the visa. Visas are granted in most cases, unless the embassy employee suspects something fishy or your fiancée can't answer simple questions (i.e. how many times you were married, how many kids you have or where you work). It is mandatory for you and your future wife to have met in person before the application process.

With this visa option you have more chances to bring your woman to your country. The main thing you have to do is convince the embassy representative during the interview that your intentions are serious and that you genuinely plan to get married and live together. An immigration officer conducting the interview might ask for proof of your correspondence as well as discuss details of your relationship, including some personal matters. You can plan to attend the interview with your bride, however, most women handle interviews well on their own.

You will have to submit the following documents to the Immigration services in the USA:

1. **I-129F form,** signed and dated.
2. **G-325A** – 2 pages from you, 2 pages from your fiancé, and 2 pages from her children if she has any, signed and dated.
3. **Original statements** - a letter from you and your fiancée whom you plan to marry within 90 days of her admission along with **copies of any evidence to prove your mutual intent** (details of your engagement, for example).

4. A copy of **your passport** – include copies of every page with stamps.
5. A copy of **your fiancé's passport** and her children, if any.
6. A copy of **divorce** certificates for you and your fiancé, if applicable, for every union (for example, if you've been married three times, you need to provide all three divorce certificates, not just the last one – this is critical).
7. Her divorce certificate must be notarized and translated by a certified translator.
8. **Birth certificate** of your lady and her children, if applicable, translated and notarized.
9. **2 passport-style color photographs** for you and your fiancé, taken within 30 days of the application date (lightly print your names on the back of each photo using a pencil or a felt pen).
10. **Evidence** of your previous meeting(s) within the last two years (photos of you together, tickets, letters).
11. **A filing fee** (currently $455, but the numbers are subject to change, so confirm the latest fees on the immigration website). The exact amount is payable by a check or money order made out to the Department of Homeland Security. If a check is made out for an account of a person other than yourself, write your name on the front of the check. If the check is not accepted, USCIS will charge a fee for the returned check.
12. **Documents to confirm a name change**, if any.

You can download all forms and instructions on filling them out at http://www.uscis.gov/forms .

Once you have collected all documents and mailed them to the immigration office, it should take about six months to get an approval letter from the immigration services. Once you've received the letter, documents will be mailed to the embassy of your country in your woman's country or to the country indicated in your documents if your fiancée wants to have interview scheduled elsewhere; your Russian bride will receive further instructions from the embassy in the mail. Interview is generally scheduled by the embassy within a month of a woman receiving initial embassy instructions. A visa is issued within a week after the interview; once she has a passport with a valid visa, she can travel to your country. Her visa will be good for 6 months, meaning she can depart anytime during this term.

You will have 90 days to decide if you want to get married from the date of your lady's arrival to the USA. If you decide to proceed, you will have to make all necessary arrangements and get married within this timeframe. If you are not married during these 90 days, she has to go back home.

You can prepare all paperwork and file the application yourself or hire an immigration lawyer. Hiring an immigration lawyer will mean additional costs, but you will have invaluable guidance and assistance at your disposal.

If you decide to handle the paperwork independently, at least invest in having an immigration consultant look through prepared documents to make sure everything is filled out correctly and all documents are in order. My fiancé filed documents for my visa independently, but forgot to submit a copy of my birth certificate; the documents were returned with a request for additional information. He saved a few hundred dollars, but we had to wait seven months longer before I could come to the USA.

The process might seem to you time consuming and complex, but do not despair – I can always direct you to a knowledgeable consultant for advice. And remember, there are no boundaries for true love.

Scenario # 3. She comes on a tourist visa; you get married while she is in the country.

Receiving a tourist visa (also called a visitor's visa) is the least recommended option, especially if your lady is trying to visit the United States of America or Europe. In order to receive a tourist visa, an applicant (your woman) has to convince the embassy that she has no reasons to become an illegal immigrant and prove that she has strong ties to her home country. This can be done by showing that she has:

- a large bank account;
- real estate investments;
- other expensive property;
- husband/children left in the country;

- high-profit job (with proof of income) which she would be unlikely to leave.

The embassy will most likely want to see a combination of these things. Since your lady is not married, she will have to provide other types of evidence. Even if your woman has all the documents in order, there is no guarantee that the embassy will grant her a visa – immigration officers have been known to refuse issuing a visa for no obvious reasons, and statistically women under 30 are least likely to be granted a tourist visa.

It is a lot easier for your woman to receive a visa if she has an invitation letter to visit someone in the US (a friend or a family member). It is not advisable for you to arrange this invitation letter because immigration officials will treat it as a potential situation for the two of you to get married or become involved in a relationship, resulting in suspicion and visa denial for your woman. It is best if your potential bride is invited by a married couple in which the husband is an American and the wife is a woman from your bride's city.

Citizens of certain countries are more likely to get a tourist or a student visa. Russians living in Moscow or St. Petersburg almost always receive such visas. Women living in large cities of Kazakhstan have very high chances of getting tourist visas. It is next to impossible for citizens of Belarus and Ukraine to receive tourist visas. This information is accurate for 2014; there might be changes in future.

Your woman can stay in the country for six months on a tourist visa – as with other visas, the term is calculated from the date she has entered the country so check the arrival stamp in her passport. You can get married during this time, provided you fell in love and felt a strong connection. Once you are married, you must submit an application for adjustment of status to the immigration department asking to change her visa from tourist to wife. The documents must be submitted before the term for her legal stay expires – before the end of six months. Once the documents are approved, she will be interviewed by an immigration officer who will grant her temporary residency status (green card).

Scenario # 4. She is already in your country on a valid visa when you decide to marry her.

Many FSU women are already living, studying, and working in the US. Most such women would have come as exchange students or on valid work or study visas. In the past, many of them chose to look for partners independently, but now most of them turn to introduction agencies for assistance. If you have met a woman who is already in your country on a valid visa and would like to marry her, this is what you can expect.

VISA TYPE	PERCENTAGE IN OKSANALOVE DATABASE	WILL YOU NEED TO FILE FOR ADJUSTMENT OF STATUS?
Tourist visa holders	15%	Yes
Business visa holders	15%	Yes
Student visa holders	10%	Yes
Residents and citizens (refugees)	20%	No
Arrived on fiancée visas (divorced)	20%	No
Hold expired visas, status unknown	20%	Yes

All these women want to create a family as soon as possible, given that they really like the man they meet. Some of them give men little time to figure out where the relationship is going; most of them will accept marriage as the only outcome. Often they will not talk about it because their Russian roots are very strong – they camouflage their emotions well and pretend not to be in a hurry to get married because they don't want to get hurt in case of rejection or freak men out.

Important INS keepsakes

When applying for a fiancée visa or for a change of status, you will have to present proof that your relationship is ongoing and genuine. To do so, you need to keep a number of things throughout your relationship to submit with K-1 visa (fiancée visa) or residency paperwork. The list below is rather basic; government officials may request additional items.

- All airplane ticket stubs and luggage tags from your travel to meet your bride;
- Receipts from your overseas purchases;
- Credit card statements showing your expenses during the trip;
- As many photos of you together during your meeting as possible;
- An engagement ring (it doesn't have to be expensive, you can always get something better later on), a receipt from your purchase, a photo of the ring in the box, a photo of it on your woman's finger;
- An original copy of your birth certificate;
- Your phone bill with her phone number highlighted for the times you called her;
- Tax returns for the last 2 years or W2;
- Your letters, copies of emails, chat screens, etc.

I would recommend buying a paper file box with 15 – 20 compartments which you will use to keep all INS paperwork. Start collecting receipts, letters, and bills, make copies of all relevant (and irrelevant) documents, make copies of the document package you submit to the immigration – INS CAN LOSE YOUR DOCUMENTS. When my fiancé submitted the paperwork, he didn't spend money on an immigration lawyer, but he did make copies of all documents we sent to the immigration. Homeland security lost my file and sent me a letter of deportation – luckily, we were able to resuscitate the process quickly thanks to the copies of all documents.

Long distance dating survival guide

As I've already said, long distance relationships are not for everyone. They often present entirely different challenges than when you are dating someone living close to you. Of course, there is no reason to panic as true feelings can overcome anything. Keeping a few simple things in mind will help you strengthen your connection with your Russian bride and make your relationship stronger thanks to the distance.

Talking on the phone or communicating every day when you are in a long distance relationship can actually do more harm than good. Keeping in touch daily (especially over phone) can create undue expectations and tension if you find that the conversation does not flow as easily some days. Of course, one can argue that being in a regular relationship people talk every day, but that is a bit different – it is much easier to have that kind of bond when you are a part of each other's daily activities. Long distance relationships – regardless of the amount and type of communication – do not give you a full picture of what your partner's daily routine is. So, when you face a situation when your partner is not as outspoken, it can make you wonder what is wrong, and since you have no way to communicate in person, your mind can run wild with guesses. That is why it is better to give each other a few days to breathe between conversations – that way when you talk, you can be sure that there will be plenty of things to discuss.

In order to keep your relationship vibrant and dynamic, do your best to plan regular trips to see each other in person while you are waiting for your documents to get approved. It doesn't matter what it is – whether you visit each other, meet on a neutral territory, or a combination of both. The main thing is that you have one-on-one time and get to see what both of you are like in regular, routine situations. Planning such visits will give both of you something to look forward to, and actual meetings will be one more way to make your bond stronger and more intimate.

Modern technology makes contacting someone overseas quick and convenient, but sometimes it is good to take advantage of the old-fashioned communication means. Sending a handwritten letter (even a note) will add a special touch to your communication. Aside from showing your lady that you take time to do something special for her, it will also give her a physical something that connects the two of you. I guarantee that your sweetheart will touch, smell, and re-read your message numerous times to feel closer to the man she cares for.

The means of communication may be many, but the essence of what is being said should not. Since most of the time you will not be able to see each other as you speak, here are a few simple tips to keep in mind to make your communication successful and expressive.

- If you have the ability to show her around – do it. Show her your house, the way you spend your days, your stores, parks, work, your daily routine, show her as much as possible (you can do that via Skype, iPhone or smartphone). This will help her feel closer to you as well as adjust to her future life with you.
- When you are telling your sweetheart about an event, a place, or a person, try to be as descriptive as possible, so she could have a good chance of imagining what it is you saw. She might not be able to read your thoughts completely, but at least she will be able to create a picture of what your day was like. The same rule goes for your feelings – in the absence of body language (seeing each other's face, eyes, etc.), put an extra effort to really explaining and sharing what you feel: if your sweetheart made you laugh, make a point of telling her that she put a smile on your face; when she says something sweet, tell her what emotions her words brought about in you. Sharing such moments will make your bond stronger.
- In addition, make sure that you exchange and share photographs and videos frequently. Seeing your face, pictures of you with your friends/family, places where you live and

visit will help your lady feel more like a part of your life. It will help her know what you talk about when you describe your life and daily activities and give her an idea of who you are.

Honesty is something to keep in mind as well. Although it is a given in any type of a relationship, being apart can be an easy way to give into temptation and make yourself sound better than you really are or someone you are not. When she finally gets to your country and some incoherencies or white lies come to light, it will be hard to regain that person's trust, and you will risk blowing a great relationship. Be honest from the beginning – it will give you an opportunity to remain true to yourself and find a partner who appreciates and loves you for who you really are.

Building a long-distance relationship and making it stronger takes work, but it is possible to make it an enjoyable experience. When you are miles apart, every word, phone call, or letter make a difference; try to always end them on a good note, and your communication will grow and become a precious gift for both of you.

Get your girl to speak English, now!

Previously we spoke about language issues – rather, the fun aspects of the matter. Up until you and your Russian bride become committed to each other, she will have the excuse of not knowing or learning the language. However, once you have made long-term plans as a couple, it becomes a whole different ball game – she no longer has excuses for not learning the language and should have all the motivation to make it her number one priority. As I've already mentioned, she will require your support, patience, and understanding, but you also must pay close attention to her progress. If you find that your lady is not devoting enough time to learning English, there can be two explanations.

1. She is plain lazy. This means you may face a number of challenges later as she will be expecting you to bear the majority of responsibilities in your relationship. Such people often have little appreciation for what is being done for them; a woman with such attitude will not make it in the US. Many

such women quickly return to their home country – no matter how hard you try to please her, there always will be "something" she doesn't like. If you notice such an attitude, you will need to set things straight from the very beginning, and if she doesn't make any changes, you might have to reconsider being in this relationship all together.

2. She has no respect for you and is not serious about your relationship. A woman in love tries to please her man, to make his life more fulfilling, to keep him happy. If she does not put effort into improving your communication through learning English, she might not have strong feelings for you. Again, if you have any doubts, you need to have a serious discussion about what is happening and make corresponding decisions.

I am not suggesting that you dump your Russian girlfriend or interrogate her weekly if she hasn't learned the language in two months. Learning a foreign language is not always easy – some people simply do not have an inclination for languages; women after 40 have an exceptionally difficult time with this. However, you must at least see that she is trying.

If your Russian bride is studying with a tutor, you may want to speak with her teacher to discuss her progress as well as find out what you can do to help. If she is using some form of language software (Rosetta Stone courses are great – they can help her learn some language basics in 3-5 months!), check out what topics it uses in the lessons and have conversations using the same vocabulary/phrases as the software – you will be able to see how much attention she pays to the lessons, and she will be comfortable because she will be repeating things she already knows.

-------------------------------- Resource! ---------------------------------
I would strongly recommend for your bride to take a class at the _www.UsaLanguageAcademy.com_ as it developed specifically for Russian women to help them learn English quickly. The program is affordable; it offers learning with a live tutor and a fun way to learn via videos and exercises. This program has been reported to show good results even from people with no language skills or learning talent.

Of course, you must encourage and support her the best you can – admire her every little achievement, do not be overly harsh or critical when correcting her, and always remind her that you love her. You must be prepared for an adaptation period full of challenges once your Russian bride arrives into your country even if she speaks English well. Several months after my arrival to the US, once I was comfortable with my English, my friends took me to see the musical "Oklahoma". I really enjoyed the play and thought I'd followed the plot exceptionally well for someone who has not had that much experience listening to American speech. The next year I attended the same play – I was shocked that the script has been changed drastically, altering the entire storyline! I was shocked even more when I was told that it has not changed a bit from the year before – it turned out that I only understood and followed about 70% of the play the previous year!

It is also a good idea to support your bride by learning a few of the words from her native tongue – this will make your communication fun and give her a chance to relax (she won't be the only one learning something new and making mistakes).

You might find interesting the story of one of my female clients. At first she didn't learn English because she didn't have any motivation – there was no man in her life. Once she met a man, she decided that Rosetta Stone software was a good option, her boyfriend bought it for her. Once she had the software, she started having computer problems, all the time. Now, two years later, she speaks very little English, her husband has been learning Russian instead, and the couple mainly communicates in Russian. I don't know many men who would be so dedicated to their women; her husband is so much in love that he doesn't care what he must do to keep his wife happy. While admirable on one hand, on another, it is a very dangerous situation – if this man ever feels slightly less affectionate (and he probably will at some point), he probably will no longer want to be so patient and giving. And frankly, I won't blame him – relationships where one partner always gives while the other person always demands never work.

At the same time, I can tell you dozens of stories when women arrived to the United States knowing just a few words of English, yet within a few months they were fluent enough to be able to communicate and understand native speakers. Being immersed in a foreign language environment puts the learning on an entirely new level - there are no translators to rely on, many things can be explained (on paper or by pointing) for easier understanding, and there is simply no other choice! Hearing television, music, and native speakers in a new language will help your lady adapt and learn the language faster. Additional language learning activities, such as English as a Foreign Language classes and various cross-cultural activities, can help build your sweetheart's confidence and gain necessary practice of a new tongue. Such programs will not only assist her in learning the language, but help your Russian bride make friends as well.

Learn to speak Russian English

It is a challenge to communicate with a Russian woman who doesn't know English, but it is an equal challenge to speak with a Russian woman who speaks the language. You must realize that most Russian people learn British English. It doesn't seem like a big deal until you find yourself in an awkward situation. During my first year in America, I once had the audacity to ask a young gentleman in a library for a rubber. I didn't understand why he gave me an awkward look, mumbled something unintelligible, and left the table rather quickly... until someone explained to me that "rubber" in America means "condom" (what I wanted was an eraser!).

You will find that Russian women often use literal translations of Russian terms or try to translate words that have a very specific meaning in Russian with no analogous terms in English. To help you eliminate some of the confusion, I offer you the list of the most common words and phrases that can help you gain a better insight into Russian mentality and understand what your lady actually means.

Create a family – literal translation from Russian which means "to get married". This does not necessarily imply children; it is acceptable to use this term to talk about the husband and wife only.

Strong family – literal translation; means a close family with harmonious relations which can withstand any challenges.

Create a cozy and comfortable home – refers to home improvement activities.

Close people – literal translation of the term used to refer to people who are special in one's life, someone you care about.

To become closer – literal translation of "get to know each other better".

Favorite man – the man I love or care for.

Real man – a man who is strong, reliable, a good provider, who can defend the woman and take care of her; someone with whom she can feel delicate and feminine.

Financially secure – this term seems to scare men quite often because they mistakenly think that a woman is looking for a rich husband. To be financially secure to Russian women means to have a stable job, a stable income with the help of which a man can provide for his family.

Provide for materially – has the same meaning as "financially secure".

Well-to-do person – this term is used when talking about people of the upper class.

Without bad habits – refers to someone who is not a drunkard, who does not smoke or do drugs.

Active rest – literal translation for "outdoor activities".

Communicative – means "sociable".

Middle education – refers to high school studies.

Higher education – literal translation for studying at a university.

Looking for the second half – literal translation of a phrase meaning that a woman is looking for a partner.

Gay – a good ole British term widely taught to be used to describe someone cheerful or happy.

Intercourse – a British word meaning "contact", "communication".

Sexual – most Russians use this word when they mean "sexy".

Intelligent – one of the most commonly misused words to describe an intellectual (or, according to the Russian language, a well-educated person with good manners, an older meaning in Russian referred to someone with a higher social status).

Manly – means "masculine".

Womanly – incorrect term for "feminine".

Orderly – when used by Russians, normally means "decent" or "faithful".

Pedagogical – usually refers to universities/establishments where one receives a degree to become a teacher.

Shaping – usually refers to fitness programs which help women improve their physical shape by toning every part of the body without becoming buff.

Sporty – means "athletic", "physically fit".

Proud – often means someone who is confident and independent.

Strong – is often used to define character quality of someone who is strong-willed as opposed to describing physical attributes.

Machine – often is misused when talking about a car, a vehicle.

Purposeful – misused to describe someone who is goal oriented.

From dating to marriage

You will never know what it takes to help someone adjust to a new culture unless you go through this process. I went through this experience when my mother and my brother moved to the US. At that time, I learned that adjustment process of young people is very different than that of someone older. Basically, it is like raising a child. You will have to be patient (very patient!), learn not to get frustrated, and take things as they come; you must understand that issues arise for a reason, and the only way to fix things is to explain to your bride the way things are done in your country. Raising your voice or getting frustrated will not help her understand things better or faster and can make her regret moving overseas in the first place.

You might think you wouldn't do any of these things, but consider this: while you were away from each other, communicating through emails, video chats or on the phone, you were in your own space, in your comfort zone. Even if you had misunderstandings or disagreements, once you disconnected, you could cool off, get yourself together, shake off all negativity and tension, and speak calmly the next day once you've had time to think about the situation and to miss your sweetheart. Now, if there is any conflict, it will be in your face; you will not have time to be away from each other and will have to deal with problems right away.

You must also be prepared that your usual routine will be disturbed. Even if you think you are ready for it, you might not be. Suddenly things will be done differently than you are used to, your wife might do things you don't understand or don't like, and you will have to adjust to her presence as much as she will have to adjust to yours (even if you love each other very much!). However, all of that will come after several days of euphoria of finally being together after the long wait.

Cultural 911: helping your Russian bride adjust

When you marry someone from your own country, you have similar traditions; you are familiar with the same books, music, holidays. When you marry a woman from abroad, your outlook on life, values, and habits will most likely be completely different. You will be able to learn something new, come to appreciate things you have in your life, and discover a whole new world thanks to learning about new culture and lifestyle. This will make your relationships more rewarding and stimulating, yet, it will also require more patience and understanding from both partners, as not being able to understand your partner 100% can be frustrating.

The first and most important thing to remember is that you are the only person your lady knows in the new country. This will require additional patience and understanding on your part as some traditions, habits, and information might be completely new to your sweetheart.

As you go through your day, just try imagining that you see everything around you for the first time: you would have no idea what each store is, what kind of food is served in each restaurant, how to get to certain places, etc. This is pretty much what things will be like for your wife when she moves to your country. There will be many things she has never seen, things she has no idea about, and you will be responsible for explaining them to her and supporting her as she learns.

If you cannot imagine the situation above, imagine this: you see a famous singer/actor you really liked growing up. This brings to your mind childhood memories, old family traditions, how you spent time with school friends. You try to share this with your partner and realize that your words mean nothing to her! Of course, she is glad to see you touched, but she does not understand what the big deal is about seeing some old guy – she has no idea how your family spent time together, she has no idea what school was like for you, she cannot relate to your memories of youth. You try to explain that this person is famous, you can't believe that she doesn't know him/her, and all your excitement and the magic of the moment give way to frustration and explanations (as you know, having to explain a joke totally ruins it!).

So, as you see, the first thing you have to store up on is patience. Do not let such misunderstandings upset you. Remember that you and your Russian wife are in the same boat: you are not able to feel why some things matter to her so much, because you do not know her country, her culture. She has her own perception of the world, and, in fact, is facing a much tougher adjustment because she is in a new place; you are still in your home country, where things are familiar to you, everyone understands you, and you have complete freedom of action, while she only has you (and perhaps your family) to talk with and learn from.

A great plus will be to have your family and friends well aware of your decision to marry someone from abroad and use their support in making your girlfriend/fiancé feel more comfortable in a new environment. Making all necessary introductions of people important in your life as early after arrival as possible will be a big plus – but make sure you give her a few days to get on schedule after jet lag and get comfortable enough for such activities. It is also a good idea to explain what is typical in your circle of family and friends – some people have a family dinner every evening to share the events of the day, others meet only at Christmas time, some people's friends play a more important role in their life than biological relatives.

The first thing you might want to do is give your lady a quick tour of the house, places visited most often (i.e. favorite store, restaurant) or the nearest city/activity center, especially if you live outside of town. This will give her an idea of where everything is located and make her feel more comfortable with the surroundings. A tour of the house might seem like a trivial thing, but it is extremely important in making your sweetheart really feel like it is her home – sometimes, not knowing where one can find trash bags or laundry soap can be frustrating, especially since most women are eager to take on responsibilities of caring for the home and creating a cozy place for the two of you. Remember to show her where toothpaste is and keep Bengay out of her reach!

When preparing for your sweetheart to arrive, you might want to buy her a small present – something that will be uniquely hers (a t-shirt, a basket with toiletries just for her, her own slippers) – to make her feel like she already has presence in your house.

And remember, cultural differences are no reason to panic. There are two simple rules to overcome them and make your relationship grow.

Rule #1. Do your research. If you met a lady from Russia, do some research on Russian culture, traditions, food, and holidays. As much useful information as you might find in this book, it is simply impossible for me to cover everything. You don't need to become a history buff, but showing that you are somewhat familiar with her country (and that you made an effort!) will make her at ease and will simplify your communication.

Rule #2. Discuss cultural things. Talk about your culture, ask about hers, ask questions, and make her do the same, show her photographs that can show what your life is/was like, share music and films that have made an impact on you and which you consider important. Seeing all these things will help your Russian bride understand you, your likes and dislikes, and will create a stronger bond based on things which are important to you. That way, next time you refer to your favorite film, your Russian bride will know exactly what you mean and why you said it. Be patient and communicate openly, and you will be able to overcome cultural differences.

New culture: Russian women and career

Among many, a common misconception some of my male clients have about Russian women is that the latter are not interested in having a career, dream to be housewives, and have no plans to work expecting their husband to take care of them for the rest of their life. This is not entirely true; just as every Russian woman is unique, so will be her needs and wants.

As you already know, most women in Russia have good education (most of them have university degrees) and take it as a given that they must work. It is usually considered a sign of wealth if a wife can stay at home. However, if a woman is ambitious and is interested in having a job not only for money, but also for the challenge, she will not want to stay at home – she might stay at home for a few months while she adjusts to a new culture, but will get bored sitting at home once she has adjusted. This has been true for nearly 80% of my female clients – after all, it takes an adventurous, active, and driven woman to look for a foreign husband and leave her home country, friends, and family.

It is a lot harder for women to establish a career in Russia because of chauvinistic tendencies, although that has been changing in the recent years. However, most vacancies, especially in management, are considered to be a better fit for men. Gender requirement is not considered discriminatory in Russia; women get paid less and have far fewer chances for career advancement. Women who make significant achievements in business have to continuously prove their worth and are constantly challenged by males in the workplace. All of these factors contribute to Russian women not being overly zealous to build grand careers unlike Western women. However, Russian women are generally very hard working, and if they have to work, they will put their best effort to it.

Establishing a career abroad can be rather intimidating to Russian women because of the language barrier. Unless her language skills are perfect, she will certainly not be thinking about finding a job in the first few months of her stay which is recommended anyway because she will need time to get adjusted to the new country, new setting, and new customs. However, once she has adjusted and gained enough confidence that she can find a job and will be able to cope with it, she might surprise you with her effort and vigor.

If your lady decides to build a career when she moves to your country, she will need you to support her throughout the process. Degrees from Russia are not recognized abroad, so your wife will most likely not be able to work in the same field as she did at home or she will require quite additional training, learning or practice before she is able to hold the same position as she did at home. For example, medical degrees from Russia are certainly not accepted abroad, and if your woman will be interested in a medical field, she will probably have to settle for a much lower position in the hospital and can definitely expect additional internships, exams, and studies before she can advance.

A lot can also depend on the family status and the age of your Russian bride. Older women seem to be more content with having modest, sometimes part-time, jobs which allow them to take care of their family in Russia as well as to contribute to the family budget. If you are marrying a younger woman, you should be prepared that she will be interested to continue her education and, naturally, go on to have a career of her own. Most women see a job as a way to keep their social and intellectual abilities sharp as well as a way to not feel completely dependent on their husband. However, most women from Russia will rarely make their career a priority and certainly will not let it get in the way of family needs (i.e. after having a baby most women will want to stay at home with the child as long as possible). Naturally, there will be some women who expect to be taken care of by their mates and will not be interested in work once married.

How can you know what to expect? The answer is very simple – bring it up in your communication/correspondence. Of course, you should be tactful. Do not say that you expect your wife to pay her own expenses; it can make a woman feel insecure, especially when she does not know if she will be able to find a job. But you can easily ask a woman you are writing to how she sees her future after marriage, if she is interested to continue her career after getting married, etc. You can tell her that you are OK either way.

If you choose not to discuss the issue prior to marriage, you should wait to discuss her possible activities and plans until your Russian bride becomes comfortable with the new home and environment. If both of you see her as a housewife, it is a good idea for her to get involved in community or charity work. If both of you are willing for her to work, she might look for a simple part-time job before moving on to something more serious. The main advantage of this approach lies in finding an activity for your lady to keep her busy (*read*: not bored and home sick), to provide language practice, to make her comfortable in the new surroundings without you by her side 24/7, and to help her meet new people.

Her answer in most cases will be that she wants to be involved in something, and very often you will find women interested in establishing their own business – something they might not have had a chance to do at home, something that might be a lot easier to set up in your country than it was in her own. It is a very good idea because she might just be able to create something unique thanks to her exposure to different culture and ideas. Normally women prefer to stay within service businesses such as a café or a restaurant, a beauty salon or a child care center.

Introducing your Russian bride to family and friends

After you and your Russian bride have been together for a while, time will come for you to introduce her to your family and friends. This can be a fairly stressful ordeal for all parties involved. Here I will give you a few suggestions on how to prepare for this occasion and make it go as smooth as possible.

You will want to make sure that everyone involved is prepared for this meeting, including your Russian bride. You can help her by discussing your family and friends long before she meets them in person. Show her their photos; describe briefly what each person is like. Tell her the most outstanding things about each member of the family – it will help her make associations to remember people better.

You may share likes and dislikes of each person, information about their families, careers, etc. It is also important to help her remember the names of the people she will be meeting – coming from a different culture it can be a challenge; helping your sweetheart remember everyone's names properly will save your sweetheart a lot of embarrassment and discomfort. If she is not fluent in the language, you should also take the time to teach her a few basic phrases or slang words which are used during small talk – it will make her feel more comfortable during the introduction. Doing all these things will help you Russian lady feel more confident because she will know what to expect.

You also must prepare your family for the meeting. Describe your sweetheart to them – share where she is from, tell them some things that you like the most about her, describe her most attractive traits, tell them how you've met. All these things will help your family and friends get to know your bride before meeting her in person and create a positive image of her because they will see her through your eyes. It is also important that you take time to talk about cultural differences. Make sure your family and friends are aware of the language issues if they exist: if your sweetheart does not know your native tongue, it will take an effort from all the native speakers (you, first of all!) to make sure she does not feel excluded from the conversation; if she has basic language skills, you might need to warn your friends and family that they should talk a bit slower, make them aware of differences in pronunciations and difficulties of understanding accents, etc. Share with them some information about the culture your sweetheart is coming from – what are some things unique to her home and family, what some of her home country traditions are, etc. It will not only make your friends and family feel like they know your Russian bride better, but also give them something to talk to her about when they finally meet.

Naturally, you will be the main conductor of the event. Being familiar with both parties, it will be up to you to make sure everything goes smoothly. Be prepared that it might be stressful and will require a lot of participation and patience on your part. Introduction of your Russian lady to your family and friends will require a lot of preliminary work from you: getting both sides acquainted with each other in advance, making sure you give both necessary information, and making sure everything goes smoothly during the introduction. For example, you will have to be the one to keep track of the conversation flow to make sure no one feels left out and minimize awkward moments. Think in advance of the things you wouldn't want your family asking your Russian lady (and vice versa) because they might be considered offensive or impolite. You might want to prepare a few things to keep on hand in order to avoid awkward pauses as well as things that can keep the conversation flowing (family picture albums are great for this purpose).

During the conversation, make sure to bring up your trip experiences in her country, remember all the funny moments you experienced while visiting her or while meeting her (if you met overseas), the memories of your first meeting will uplift her spirit as you will be talking about moments when you first fell in love. If you speak of funny moments you and your bride shared during your meetings, she will feel quite at home during the conversation even if she doesn't speak much English as she will know what you are talking about.

When telling your friends and family about your travel experience, speak highly of people who are close to her and make sure you are ready to pick and up where she stumbles, make sure to encourage her when she makes mistakes, forgets words, or uses phrases incorrectly. Do not be critical of her during this time – this will be 10 times harder for her than it would be under normal circumstances because she will be very nervous wanting to be accepted and make a good impression on your family.

Easy ways to ruin your marriage

Most men wanting to marry a Russian woman have no idea what the world is like through her eyes. While you might know that things in your country will be pretty unusual for her, you cannot imagine how many new things she will face and how she will deal with them. Below I list a few things you should be prepared for when you bride arrives to your country.

Credit. This is a big deal, you must explain to your bride how credit cards work and what credit history means. Even though former Soviet countries have been introducing use of credit in the recent years, it is processed and treated quite differently than in the US. If you do not explain how this concept works, you might end up with a ruined credit history (trust me, I've seen it happen more than once!). If you think you can hide credit cards from her – think again: there always will be a girlfriend in America who will "teach" her to use credit cards.

Driver's license and social security. You need to explain what both these things are. In Russia and neighboring countries, a passport is the main means of identification; individual national code (similar to social security number) is used for many things, including bank paperwork, big purchases, etc.

Driving. Even if she has a license in Russia, she will be very cautious driving in your country. She will be endlessly surprised by the quality of the roads (in a good way) and get nervous every time she sees a police car. She will find it a pleasant surprise to drive on straight roads without potholes, where everyone follows the rules and police don't ask for bribes if they stop you even without your fault. She will probably stick with the back roads for a few months and will think she is not brave enough to drive on an expressway with all that traffic!

Schooling system. In Russia there is free and paid education. Paid educational programs are not nearly as expensive as they are abroad. Parents pay for their children's education 99% of the time. Unless you plan to do the same, you need to explain how things work and discuss this issue with her before you have children, otherwise she might be offended and upset when she finds out that you are not going to fund your children's education. School system is completely different – in Russia, students never select their courses, whether they attend a high school or a university.

Prenuptial agreements. This is a hot topic that needs to be addressed correctly. You should protect your assets, no doubt. Most Russian women sign prenups without a problem, but you need to explain things correctly and tactfully. All of my female clients with whom I discussed the issue signed a prenup without a second thought.

Dress code. Foreign men like the fact that Russian women wear short skirts and sexy dresses; however, they often don't like seeing Russian women wear the same outfits once they come to their men's country. You need to address the issue, but, please, be delicate and tactful.

Appliances. You already know that many people wash dishes (sometimes clothes too) by hand. Your bride will take time getting used to appliances and the comfort of using a dish washer, a dryer, and other things that make household duties so much easier. Women often think the reason for using so many appliances is that Americans are lazy and don't want to get their hands dirty; Russian are, on the contrary, tough and hardworking, so they don't need to use all this fancy stuff. Because of such thinking, they will often criticize the use of so many appliances and want to do things the way they did them at home. You must explain to your bride that these things will not diminish her input towards taking care of the house and will, in fact, give her an opportunity to have more time to do other things that are more important and exciting.

Being friendly. Russians are very hospitable to everyone who comes to their home, but they are not used to being friendly and open to strangers on the streets. You need to explain that people can smile without any reason. You also need to find a way to explain to her that she can't cut in front of others and she doesn't have to push other people out of the way in a grocery store as she might have had to do back at home.

Getting everything without doing anything. This is a horrible stereotype Russians have about Americans; they think Americans don't need to do anything to get the good things in life, and that everything is served to them on a gold platter. Russian women are used to buying things by paying cash, even when it comes to big purchases. When you speak of "your" house, she will most likely think that you would have paid for it and are the owner of the property. To avoid an awkward situation (like your bride thinking that you lied to her when you spoke about "your" home), discuss such issues well in advance, so she knows exactly what she is getting herself into.

Sales. Sales have only started to become common and popular in Russia and former Soviet countries in recent years. Most Russians still think that buying discounted items is shameful, as if they are getting lower grade products, or that only poor people buy items on sale. Because living in America will mean a higher quality of life than that in her home country, your bride might think that she now has to buy things only at full price to reflect the change in social status. She might also think that if you buy things on sale, you must be stingy or greedy. You need to explain to her what is good and bad about sales and discuss some ground rules for using the family budget.

Cell phones, Internet services, landlines. You need to explain to your bride how your cell phone, landline, and Internet services work – what you pay for them, how much minutes/gigabytes you are allowed, which services are most suitable for particular needs. In Ukraine, for example, many monthly Internet packages offer unlimited use. As a contrasting example, many of my male clients ended up with bills for thousands of dollars at the end of the month simply because they didn't explain to their bride the costs of calling her country via telephone.

Phone calls. Your Russian bride will most likely be afraid to… answer the phone because of her lack of confidence in her English skills. Don't pressure her, don't rush; after a few months she will be able to understand the fluent speech of native speakers and will enjoy talking on the phone (feel sorry for the unsuspecting telemarketers who will become her practice targets!).

Abuse. You need to explain to your woman that it is not okay for her to… abuse you. Yes, I am serious. You will find that many couples in Russia solve their disagreements in a rough manner, including women slapping their man, screaming at him, breaking dishes (sometimes against his head). Sadly, it happens because that's what they've learned from their grandmothers and mothers. Some of the girls from my agency who married American men ended up in police custody and were clueless as to why it happened. When it happened, they also considered their husbands to be cowards, because in Russia it is dishonorable for a man to admit that he was hit by his wife (he is not a real man if he can't handle his woman). Naturally, it is not okay for a husband to abuse his wife, but that goes without saying.

Law. You need to make sure that your Russian wife knows that people actually abide by the law in your country. Remember, she comes from a country where bribes are common; almost any problem can be solved with the help of money. When I first started driving in America, I tried bribing a cop. He explained to me that it was illegal, but I thought he was simply driving a hard bargain and offered him a larger sum. It never occurred to me that it really was illegal and frowned upon, and that a police officer actually had the integrity not to take the bribe. Luckily for me, this particular officer has dealt with foreigners before and realized that it was a cultural misunderstanding, instead of throwing me into jail.

Taxes. Filing taxes will be weird for your bride because such issues are solved under the table by paying cash in her country. She might even give you "suggestions" on how you can avoid it.

World War II. If you know what's good for you, you will avoid this topic altogether. Russians are very emotional about World War II – it is considered the greatest victory in the history of Russian people. Almost every Russian woman has a grandfather or a grandmother who was affected by the war. People of Russia, Ukraine, and Belarus suffered greatly from the fascist regime, memories of the events are very painful even for younger people, and Russian history books don't necessarily portrait Americans as heroes. What you learned at school about the event will probably be radically different to what your Russian bride would have learned. I've known couples who came on the verge of break-up after discussing the issue, and I don't know a single couple that hasn't ended up arguing when discussing WWII. So, if you want to enjoy a happy future with your Russian wife, be the wise one and don't discuss this subject.

Russian food, Russian stores. She will probably make dishes you will find strange. For example, a salad called "herring under a fur coat" (salty herring covered with layers of cooked vegetables). I haven't met an American who could try it without disgust. Your wife might very well get offended if you don't like what she cooks. It is a good idea to discuss food preferences and to agree to disagree when it comes to some dishes. Make sure to tell her not to take it personally if you don't enjoy some of her Russian inspired creations. Your Russian wife will really enjoy shopping at Russian stores, if she finds any; she will think that food from such shops is more organic and is better for you. Whether she is right or not, respect her roots and wishes of having strange dishes she enjoys, even if you don't.

Food. Your Russian bride might have never seen an artichoke or a sweet potato. She probably (most likely) will not like peanut butter. She will be stunned seeing the amount of food in the grocery stores, but she will not be able to find things she "needs": *tvorog* – Russian variety of cottage cheese, *seledka* – marinated herring, etc. This means that she will start looking for Russian stores or restaurants. Be prepared to become somewhat of a guinea pig who will be required to taste everything she cooks (see the paragraph above on how to handle this). She will not like store-bought bread, unless she can find a small private bakery that does it "the right way" – by the way, having a bread maker can be a very pleasant surprise for your wife.

Many Russians also think that all American food items are genetically modified, full of hormones and harmful additives. If you are not shopping in stores that offer organic foods, you probably will begin to do so after your wife arrives – she will argue with you until she is blue in the face that it is good for you and that she wants you to be healthy and live a long life, which means that you probably will have to buy organic food every now and then.

Miscellaneous. She will take a long time to get ready trying to keep her makeup and hair flawless. She will wear a fancy dress and high heels just to go to a grocery store. She will get excited when she meets other Russians in the area and will chatter away to them in Russian as if they've known each other for years. She will carry a camera with her and take photos of the most unexpected things to send to her friends and relatives (I know a girl who photographed a toilet with an automatic flushing system).

Naturally, there will be many other instances of cultural differences which you and your wife will have to overcome. They can be fun, they can be frustrating, they can be shocking, but so long as you discuss everything and remember how much you love each other, you will get through all challenges.

As I've already mentioned, my mother and brother adapted to the new country quite differently – the older the person, the harder it is for them to adjust. My brother, for example, accepted the new lifestyle very quickly. My mother, on the other hand, criticized many things (still does) because they were not done "the right way". It is taking her years to understand this country better and get used to the way things are done here. If your bride is over 40, be prepared that it will take her quite some time to adjust, you will need to be extra patient, and it will take her a long time to learn the language.

-------------------------------- Resource! ----------------------------------
Many couples have found the adjustment process to be a huge challenge which is why many of my male clients have been asking me for assistance. I created a program based on my knowledge and experiences of hundreds of my former clients which is called "Quick adjustment to the USA". If you want to minimize your frustration, avoid hours of discussions and arguments, this is your solution. By purchasing this program for your bride, you will be letting me do all the explaining and cultural training (all materials are in Russian). I am adding some final touches to the material, but you can check out what I have so far at www.OksanaLove.com . This program will get your woman ready for life in the US before she even arrives.

When your Russian bride is homesick

You need to be ready to deal with her homesickness. The best way to handle this is to come up with a way for your Russian wife to communicate with her family frequently. Have this worked out before she comes so that she could contact them right after her arrival – it will help her make the transition easier. Make sure that you explain to her the best options for keeping in touch (i.e. email is ok anytime, but phone calls are expensive and are ok only twice a month).

You can distract her from feeling homesick by doing something fun and pleasant:

- Take her somewhere that will make her feel like she is back home (a Russian restaurant, a Russian shop).
- Organize a romantic picnic or prepare a home-cooked dinner for her as opposed to eating out. It will show your Russian

bride or wife that you are prepared to go an extra mile for her – any woman will appreciate such gesture.

- Many Russian women enjoy art. Take your woman to a theatre, an exhibit or another cultural event where you can spend a day together. Don't forget about lunch in a quiet café to complete your date.
- Arrange a romantic evening for her with many candles (not too scented though), flower petals (on the floor, on the bed, in a bath), and a relaxing massage. Don't forget to switch off the phones so your conversation and time together is not interrupted.

Five years from now...

A few years down the road things will be quite different:

- She will go wherever and whenever she wants to paying little attention to police vehicles and feeling at home on any freeway.
- She will spend hours on the phone talking to her new friends and get annoyed with telemarketers just like everyone else.
- She will know how to cook sweet potatoes, make stuffing, and other traditional dishes. She will visit Russian food stores on a rare occasion... but she still will not like peanut butter or bread sold in stores.
- She will get dressed up only if the occasion demands it, and will certainly wear jeans and t-shirts when going to the store.
- She will not be able to imagine her life without a dishwasher and a dryer.
- She will feel quite at home and will forget to take pictures to send home even when she should.
- She will be paying taxes and reproach people who try to take advantage of the system.
- She will speak perfect English... so much you might start missing the days when she only knew a few words.

Now you are ready to deal with anything that might come your way while you are looking for a wonderful, beautiful, smart, loving, unique Russian woman – and you know that it is not that complicated.

You know that Russian women are delicate, tender, sexy, caring, yet very strong in spirit and able to overcome any difficulties. They know how to love, how to make their men feel like kings, how to stay devoted and loyal no matter how hard the times are. Such women are worth pursuing – they are worth fighting for. These women are more addictive than drugs – once you spend time with them, you will never want anyone else. Russian women know how to inspire, how to help their men do amazing things and achieve any of their dreams. A Russian bride is everything you ever dreamed of, she is everything you need and more – and she is waiting for you.

Let's go find her!

Bonus: Scam me NOT

Let me tell you how I became unintentionally "introduced" to dating scams (some of this information has been published on my website and has helped thousands of men to save money and to avoid becoming a scam victim).

Ten years ago I landed in a small airport of a cozy and sunny Lugansk, a Ukrainian suburban city. A beautiful, slim flight attendant with a glowing smile wished all the passengers a wonderful time in this amazing Ukrainian city with rich history and original culture.

I arrived to open a new office of "Oksanalove" in the city. I was not sure why I was attracted to this small Ukrainian city – after all, there were so many big cities in other countries where Russian girls were searching for their prince. It must have been the rumor that the city is full of hot and sensual Ukrainian girls, every one of whom can be a supermodel, but it turned out true. Later I found out why it was so: many years ago, the Russian Empress Ekaterina II exiled all beautiful women from her surroundings to a remote area so that their beauty would not overshadow her own. It so happened that all these unbelievable beauties were sent to the unknown city of Lugansk, where they passed their genes to many future generations. It sounds like a beautiful legend, but one starts believing it when walking down the streets of Lugansk and seeing the dazzling smiles of its beauties.

On one of the hot days, while I was taking a break from all my dealings with notaries and administrative officials of the city, I ended up on a bench in the shadow of a pretty cozy park and was lazily observing the people close to me. A group of four – two men and two women – attracted my attention. One of the women was tremendously beautiful! An athletic guy was by her side, and he was looking in a very unfriendly way at the other gentleman in the group who kept looking at the beautiful girl with unconcealed admiration and spoke English. The other woman in the group was a translator, as I understood later, and seemed nervous and diffident. The beauty was only answering "yes" or "no", the conversation she was having with the foreigner seemed more like a monolog. After 15-20 minutes, the foreigner got a few notes from his wallet and handed them to the translator, while the two women and the athletic chap got in a car and left.

I decided to approach the dishevelled foreigner to see if he needed any help. I learned that he was an American and was very confused – from that moment I learned about a different side of Lugansk, I learned the shocking truth about the city.

The American gentleman's name was Steve. He traveled from the USA to meet his virtual dream woman and to start a family with her. His family was expecting him home with his beautiful, loving, and caring Ukrainian bride. However, Steve's fiancé disappeared from his life unexpectedly, just as she entered it. The same fate befell his friend who came to Lugansk with him. So, what was so horrible and what happened to both of them?

I won't go into personal details, but will share with you just the basics that were confirmed, to my horror, by the manager of my newly registered Lugansk branch of "Oksanalove" after I related Steve's story to her.

There is a number of fake introduction agencies in Lugansk. They do not release their contact details, they do not provide clients with trustworthy information, they do not advertise. They place photos of beautiful women (their "clients") on free dating websites. Many of these women are married and remain faithful to their husbands. How, you might ask? They don't come to the agency to find a partner or to cheat on their spouses; they come to the agency to... make money!

No, they are not prostitutes. All they do is bring their photos to the agency and let them do the rest. The agency employees then decide on which website to place the photos, they write letters from a woman's name, making foreign men believe that the woman is in love with them and wants a relationship. Foreign men fly to Lugansk on the wings of love to see their beloved fiancé, they meet her and... get brushed off instead of receiving a warm welcome. At the same time, they pay all expenses for a translator, a driver, an apartment selected for them, and whatever else they might be told to pay for by the agency. Their brides, of course, share profits with the agency, usually getting a percentage of the entire sum spent by their foreign "fiancés", and, therefore, are interested in stimulating them to be as generous as possible.

Unfortunately, this is not a myth – I personally investigated and checked this information while in the city. I attended two agencies pretending to be an interested client and received detailed explanation about how things work and what would be expected of me as a potential "bride", despite the fact that I was married, as I told the employees of these agencies not to arouse any suspicions. Learning these frightening details only fueled my desire to create a real, legal, professional agency to help truly interested women meet truly interested men. I opened my office in Lugansk shortly thereafter.

Based on my research and statistics of my agency, scammers often operate in small cities, those with population under 500 000 inhabitants (yes, in Russia it is considered a small city). So, Lugansk is considered a scam capital of Ukraine and Yoshkar Ola is considered a scam capital of Russia. You also will find many scammers operating in Zaporozhye, Ukraine.

Over the years, I've met so many men who became scam victims. Sometimes these men would just walk into my agency off the street and share their stories, other times I learned from my current clients about scams they'd faced prior to coming to my agency.

Often, men would travel overseas to meet the lady they've been writing to for weeks to find out that she doesn't want to meet him in person or that she doesn't even exist – these men would then be stuck for two weeks in a foreign country without anyone to accompany them. Other men share horror stories of being tricked into paying hundreds or thousands dollars, many times for women's passports, visas that were never processed, and tickets that were never bought. I've heard of men who had sent 40-50K to their "sweethearts" to help them pay for a "surgery" of a family member who, of course, was not sick at all. And, of course, there have been numerous cases of men being greeted upon their arrival by women claiming to be the ones they've been corresponding with, but looking nothing like their sweetheart.

So, what causes women of Russia and Ukraine to become scam artists? The truth is rather sad: their willingness to deceive is often dictated by desperation – some young women have no other way to earn extra income as salaries and scholarships do not provide adequate means of living. And, of course, they choose this option because it guarantees a fairly reasonable income with least effort.

You might find some statistics interesting. Just about 10 years ago most scammers were in their 20's. Often 18 year old girls would pursue men in their 60's and 70's, convincing them that such young women could fall in love with them. Now, I don't have a problem with a big age difference in relationships – love truly conquers all, but when a 20-year-old woman tells a 60-year-old man in her third letter that she is in love... Seriously, would common sense not tell you that something is wrong with this picture? Yet, men, reasonable and sensible men, fall for this without a second thought. Of course, it is possible for a 20-year-old girl to fall in love with 60-year-old man, but it would certainly take more than three letters – it takes time to get to know each other, to build a relationship through correspondence and personal meetings and to build trust.

Now the situation has slightly changed: most scammers are between ages of 30 and 50, the majority of them being around 35. While most men have learned to stay away from very young women and decided to be smart by paying more attention to women in their 30's and 40's, scammers have followed the trend, and now it is middle-aged women that deceive foreign men.

Honestly, I can talk for hours about scams, how they work, and who becomes involved in them. The entire scam phenomena has interested me so much that I not only monitor women at my agency very closely and eliminate any scammers at the first signs of suspicious activity, but I also continue to gather information about various scams and individuals or agencies involved. Over the years, I've collected a lot of material which, I am sure, you will find interesting and beneficial.

Just recently, purely by accident, I met a woman who used to work at an agency that operated by scamming foreigners. As she is no longer associated with that agency, she has agreed to share exclusive information about her experience as a scam artist which I offer you in a special webinar. In fact, meeting Kate and seeing the overwhelming response from my clients and men who participated in the webinar prompted me to take my interest in busting scams a step further – I have decided to publish a book which will contain everything I know about scams, including effective strategies on how to avoid them. To find out more about the book "Scam me NOT", visit www.oksanalove.com/rbscam and enter your email to download a free chapter of the book and for a chance to win a free copy of it.

Afterword

Thank you for giving me the opportunity to share with you my viewpoint on finding and marrying your perfect lady – YOUR Russian Allure.

What do you want the most? Having a harmonious relationship? To find an ideal match for you, a woman who is traditional, loving, passionate, beautiful inside and out? To find a woman who would really love you for who you are? In truth, we all long for the same overwhelming human reward: understanding, appreciation, and respect. I understand you, I appreciate you, and I respect you. And I know that I can help you find true love you been looking for. I hope you've seen this on the pages of the book and will want to move ahead from simply reading my book to having a solid, happy relationship.

Be sure to check the back of this book for two special offers and resources. I hope you will take advantage of both.

I want to thank you and your agency, for your exception help on meeting and arranging our meeting for me and Oksana. I want to notify you that Oksana and me are now happily married and please see our photos. Your matchmaking and organization of our dates was a wonderful experience that I would advise all men to rely on your services and your expertise. You truly a professional at what you are doing and every man should trust your judgment like I did. Lex and Oksana

Thank you for all your help to meet my Lyudmila! I didn't really expect that something like this could really happen.

I'd love in the least to keep you apprised of everything and let you know when she gets here I'll be able to have some pictures of her in a wedding dress. Thank you for all assistance and help on meeting my Mila! Garen

I will admit that at first I was a bit skeptical regarding the possibility that I could meet my "dream girl" from Russia. Although, this was my thinking at the time I went ahead and flew to Punta Cana. On my first trip I did not meet anyone that I really clicked with. I returned to Punta Cana two more times and each time it gave Oksana time to get to know me and the type of woman I was looking for, and the type of guy I am, so that she was able to match me up with someone that I would be compatible with. On my third trip Oksana Introduced me to the most wonderful, amazing, sweet, beautiful, perfect match for me....she introduced me to my "Dream Girl"!!!! I am engaged now to the woman I have waited a lifetime to meet. I could not be happier!! Thank you Oksana, Jeff

TO HELP YOU GET A FULL VALUE FROM THIS BOOK, THERE IS A COLLECTION OF

FREE EXTRA RESOURCES:

Waiting for you at www.OksanaLove.com (available right after free profile registration):

Free video course "The Path to the Russian Heart" reveals

• **Russian girls are the best in camouflaging their feelings and real thoughts.** *Learn to "read" her.*

• **The most HATED word by Russian women – a word that is a deal breaker of your potential relationship.**

• **Many Russian women would consider an older man for a husband. Here is why...** *7 major reasons, including a shocking psychological cause*

• **Sexuality of Russian women, and what's up with that?**

PLUS

Visit www.OksanaLove.com to instantly access OKSANA LIVE TV – free weekly video interviews of real Alluring women of OksanaLove.com mixed with video episodes about dating, travel, and love advice. As a host of OKSANA LIVE TV, Oksana will share with you the most valuable, up-to-date video advice on how to attract, meet, court, and marry your Russian Allure today.

FREE OFFERS FROM OKSANA BOICHENKO

TO HELP YOU MEET QUALITY WOMEN TODAY

<u>Special Free Gift # 1 from the Author:</u>

FREE WALL CALENDAR WITH THE MOST BEAUTIFUL WOMEN MEN LIVE FOR WHOM YOU ARE ENTITLED TO DATE TODAY

In the Calendar you will see real most alluring, loving, passionate and traditional women you can ask out on a DATE TODAY.

Visit www.OksanaLove.com/GIFT to register your free profile and enter promo code **FREE416** in the "Promo Code" field to get:

3. Your free wall calendar with 12 beautiful Russian women of my agency (shipped to your door).

4. The ULTIMATE Insider Secrets booklet containing in depth background information about all 12 women (shipped with the calendar).

Special Free Gift # 2 from the Author:

FREE FIRST CHAPTER OF THE BOOK

Russian Allure: "SCAM ME NOT"

Revealed in the book:

- 3 most popular sites where you will run into scammers.
- 2 most frequently used scam schemes
- Training boot camp that creates professional scammers
- Scammer profiles
- Inside operations of scam agencies
- Letter templates con artists use to get your money
- "Wages" of scammers
- 7 simple steps to check if your Russian woman is real
- How to determine the difference between a real Russian Allure and a fake

And much more.

Meet my guest # 1 **Interview in the book**– a scam agency manager Kate. She has been scamming men just like you for many years, and today she will reveal the naked truth of what's happening inside this "business" and how scammers operate to squeeze funds out of men just like you.

The information included in the book is a MUST HAVE resource for every man who is considering finding a beautiful Russian wife.
Go to www.OksanaLove.com/rbscam and enter your email to claim your free gift - first chapter of the book "Scam me NOT". You will also be automatically enrolled to win a free copy of my book.